HOW TO BE A FIX-IT GENIUS USING 7 SIMPLE TOOLS

JOHN STOCKWELL
AND
HERBERT HOLTJE

McGRAW-HILL BOOK COMPANY
NEW YORK ST. LOUIS SAN FRANCISCO
AUCKLAND DÜSSELDORF JOHANNESBURG KUALA LUMPUR
LONDON MEXICO MONTREAL NEW DELHI PANAMA
PARIS SÃO PAULO SINGAPORE SYDNEY TOKYO TORONTO

Library of Congress Cataloging in Publication Data
Stockwell, John.
  How to be a fix-it genius using 7 simple tools.
  Includes index.
  1. Dwellings—Maintenance and repair—Amateurs'
manuals. I. Holtje, Herbert, joint author. II. Ti-
tle.
TH4817.3.S78   643'.7   75-16259
ISBN 0-07-061587-X

1234567890 HDBP 784321098765

The editors for this book were Leonard Josephson and
Patricia A. Allen, the designer was Richard A. Roth,
and the production supervisor was Teresa F. Leaden.
It was set in Century by University Graphics, Inc.

It was printed by Halliday Lithograph Corporation
and bound by The Book Press.

CONTENTS

Floors • Repairing Tile Floors • Patching Sheet Floors •
Stairs • Squeaking Stairs • Stair Safety • Refinishing
Stairs

INTRODUCTION

WE ONCE HAD twenty thumbs—ten per author. Now we have four—just two each. How we managed to attain this state is really what this book is all about.

We were charter members of the Thumbmashers' Club which met regularly every Saturday morning at the local hardware store. The owner got rich; we got leaks, shocks, cuts, and funny noises in the night. The owner bought himself a home in the country; we bought every tool he stocked, and still had trouble with the toilets.

When the owner bought a boat, we called it quits.

Surely, we reasoned, our ancestors didn't leave their caves by discovering fire and a set of chromium-plated socket wrenches. Rather, civilization was built with *simple tools*. And, if simple tools could keep a cave from leaking and a saber-toothed tiger away from the door, then surely simple tools could fix our toilets and protect us from termites.

Hence this book.

Our discovery seems so obvious now. We thought tools could substitute for common sense. Like sirens, these gleaming tools beckoned us each weekend; they seduced us to the point where our pocketbooks were thin and our thumbs were swollen.

Then one day we met Tore, a legendary Scandinavian carpenter, buying a bag of nails. We envied him and wished we could line him up to do all the building and fixing jobs that lay ahead of us. But this we couldn't do. His waiting list was long, and most of our jobs seemed urgent. So we settled for something next to best: we would show Tore that we were a couple of old pros handling a hammer with the best of them.

"What do you think of this, Tore?" one of us asked, waving a strange little gadget from the counter.

"What's that?" he responded with an arch of the brow.

"It's the greatest little thing for finding studs in the wall when you want to hang something heavy," we explained.

"I just thump the wall with my fist," said Tore, and he paid for his nails.

That was the beginning of our revelation.

We started to question the need for all those shiny tools we kept accumulating. Soon, we posed a challenge to ourselves: *How many jobs could you do around the home if you had to limit yourself to a few simple tools?*

As we tossed this question back and forth, it became clear that many common repair jobs likely to be faced by a person living in a house or an apartment could be handled successfully—*and expertly*—by the beginner with no more than seven simple tools. These were the tools sifted out by this research:

1. A hammer
2. A pair of pliers
3. A monkey wrench
4. A saw with interchangeable blades
5. A 4-inch wall scraper
6. A ratchet screwdriver with assorted bits
7. An ordinary plunger or plumber's friend

We were absolutely dazzled by the proportions of our discovery. Here were seven simple tools that could turn the most unhandy person into a tower of confidence, transform helpless dabblers into self-assured models of expertise, and free people from fearsome superintendents and expensive mechanics.

For less than 20 dollars, you can buy quality versions of the seven tools we mentioned. Most of them can be stored in a kitchen drawer; the plunger can go under the sink. These tools, together with common household items you already own—such as a knife, a can opener, a coat hanger, and a block of wood—will enable you to tackle at least 90 percent of the repair jobs facing the average person. You'll be able to build useful things, too. And, you'll save the time, money, and annoyance of dealing with the increasingly scarce repair people.

Most important, you'll probably do a better job yourself, and gain the pride and satisfaction that come to every handy person when he or she finally realizes there is nothing to fear under the sink or behind the switch plate.

In trying this book out on a number of unhandy friends, we discovered that the only thing keeping these people from enjoying all the benefits we outlined is their unfounded fear that repair jobs are terribly complicated and beyond ordinary understanding. Nothing could be farther from the truth.

In these pages, we hope to demolish that thought in you, and to encourage you to join the ranks of the formerly unhandy who are now liberated from leaks, drips, squeaks, and all the assorted annoyances of living in a home.

The seven simple tools.

Chapter 1

THE SEVEN BASIC TOOLS

WE'RE WILLING TO BET that you have at least one, and most probably several, repair or maintenance projects facing you right now. And if you're like most of us, you've probably become quite skillful at finding reasons for putting off these jobs. Welcome to the club!

The number 1 reason for this stalling is the dread of tackling something you feel is beyond your ability. Just as important is the almost universal feeling that you need special or expensive tools. Bunk to both these reasons!

We want to take a minute or two at the beginning to reassure you that the skills needed to do 95 percent of your home repair jobs can be learned quickly and easily by anyone. If you can drive a car or push a vacuum cleaner, you can learn to use simple tools and handle hundreds of repair jobs like a professional.

WHY SEVEN TOOLS?

Even the most unhandy of our readers probably has more than the seven tools kicking around in various drawers, bins, and closets. However, they usually make a weird collection once they are gathered together. For example, we've seen a neighbor's collection that included a hammer with one claw missing, a beautiful 24-inch wrench that needed a husky steamfitter just to lift, a screwdriver with a broken handle, and not a pair of pliers in sight.

The point is simply this: Most tool collections in the average household have been acquired over the years with no thought whatever to the various jobs for which they will be used. The seven simple tools that we will discuss are a "householder's survival kit." By survival kit we mean they are the minimum number of tools that will enable you to handle the maximum number of household emergencies. It's that simple. Here are the tools:

Hammer

For a simple tool, there are many different types of hammer available. They vary in size, weight, design, purpose, and materials. For the average person the best choice is a 13-ounce curved-claw hammer. The 13 ounces refers to the weight of the head. A small tack hammer might weigh 7 ounces, while a professional carpenter may prefer a heavier 16- or 20-ounce hammer for ordinary construction.

Handles come in different materials. Wood handles have a nice feel in your palm; they absorb the shocks of nailing, but will eventually dry out and loosen in the head. A metal handle is part of the head forever, but some people dislike the feel. Our advice is to heft a few different ones and pick the most comfortable.

The curved claw is best for pulling out nails. If you happen to own an old house and you figure on doing a lot of ripping and tearing of old woodwork, then consider a heavier hammer with a straight claw. The straight claw can be used as a sort of minicrowbar for pulling off old trim, lath, and paneling.

The following may seem like a blinding glimpse of

Hold the hammer near the end, and use your whole arm in swinging it.

the obvious, but there is a right way and a wrong way to use a hammer. Most beginners are afraid to swing. They grip the hammer halfway up the handle and use only a halfhearted wrist motion. Hold the hammer near the bottom of the handle and use a free swinging motion that comes from your elbow and shoulder. In

A small block of wood under the head makes it easy to withdraw a nail.

this way, you can handle a hammer all day long without tiring.

Never use a hammer with a loose head or a face that is chipped. If the face is chipped, it usually means defective heat treating or just a cheap hammer. In either case you're taking a risk the next chip may go into your eye.

When you hammer, keep your eye on the nail. It's much like golfing, where you must keep your eye on the ball. Start a nail by giving it a few very light taps to get it in position in the wood. You shouldn't have to take more than three or four more swings to drive the nail home. If it takes more, you're being shy about swinging that forearm.

You can ruin a hammer if you use it improperly. Don't use the cheek (the side of the hammer) to drive nails or to strike hard objects.

Buy a good hammer and it will outlast you. A good hammer is slightly bell-shaped on the striking face. This prevents gouging or marring the surface of the wood when you strike your final blow. Pick a major brand of one of the famous tool houses and you won't go wrong.

Pliers

Pliers seem to be a challenge to tool designers. A brief look at a tool catalog will show a variety of pliers that can intimidate even the most confident do-it-yourselfer. But fortunately there is one basic design that can be used for just about every simple home repair job: the slip-joint plier.

As the name implies, there is a joint at the pivot point which allows the plier to be set for either a normal or a wider opening. This adjustment also permits the user to get greater leverage from the handles, depending on the size of the work being held.

Slip-joint pliers come in several sizes, and it is best not to get a pair which measures less than 6 inches

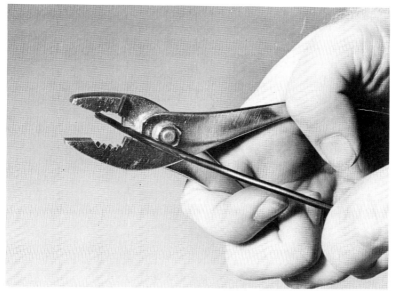

Slip-joint pliers can cut fairly heavy wire if you use the jaws near the pivot screw.

from the tip of the jaws to the end of the handle. Pliers measuring around 8 inches are ideal because they will give good leverage for tight work. And be sure to look at the point where the jaws come together. The pliers you want should have flat faces that can be used to cut wire also.

Don't buy a cheap pair of pliers. The price difference between a good pair and a cheap pair is not that great, and when you consider what it costs to replace the cheap pair when it breaks, you're ahead of the game buying quality at the start. It's hard to tell a cheap pair from a good pair just by looking, but remember this: A good pair of pliers is made from *forged* steel, and most good pliers will have this message imprinted on their handles. Inexpensive pliers are often made of castings and will break when used for much more than cracking walnuts. If in doubt, ask the hardware dealer. If the dealer isn't sure—don't buy. Find another store where you can be sure that you are getting a good tool.

Basically, pliers are used to hold anything that can't be held or turned by hand. The slip-joint plier will open to accommodate wide work, and it can be used to cut wire. The tips of the jaws are flat for holding work requiring such a grip, while the inner jaws are serrated and concave to hold round work like pipe and valve stems. You can also use the inner jaws to turn nuts and bolt heads.

The farther back on the handles you hold the pliers, the better the leverage you will get with far less muscle power, and with less chance of getting your hand pinched at the joint. If you're trying to hold something that may be marred by the teeth of the pliers, place some adhesive tape on the face of the jaws. The tighter you plan to grip, the more layers of tape should be applied.

Combination Spiral-Ratchet Screwdriver

While this handy tool is almost always referred to as a screwdriver, it is really a combination screwdriver and drill. Simply pushing down on this tool will cause the head of the screwdriver to turn and either drive a screw or drill a hole, depending on the tip you use. The tips are easily interchangeable; most manufacturers who make this tool also make complete kits of tips which include flat-blade screwdrivers, tips for Phillips-head screws, plus a set of standard-size drill points. It is even possible to get a countersinking tip which allows you to drill a small conical hole so that you can sink screws flush with surfaces.

Don't scrimp on this tool. Get the best all-purpose model the particular manufacturer offers. And be sure to get a model with an automatic return. This model has a built-in spring so that the blade stays in the slot as the handle is raised for another stroke. Also, make sure that it has a three-position lever which allows you to lock the blade or use it to drive or loosen.

One of the things that seems to confuse buyers of this tool is the number of different types of handles available. Find the handle that is most comfortable. But in the interest of simplicity, give thought to a model which has the tips stored right in the handle.

Getting the hang of using a spiral-ratchet screwdriver takes only a few minutes, but in that time, it is possible to give yourself a nasty blood blister if you get your fingers caught between the metal parts on the downstroke. A minute or two of light practice will make you a blisterless pro.

When using the spiral-ratchet screwdriver with

Steady the end of the screw driver to keep it from slip - ping out of the slot and pos- sibly marring your work.

drill points, you should be especially careful to hold the drill in the same position as it is pushed down. This downward motion often moves the drill off center, and when the drill has taken a deep enough bite, it is possible to break the point.

Other than that, keep the shank lightly oiled and the spiral-ratchet screwdriver will turn out to be one of your most practical tools.

Turret Saw

Most home repair jobs require some cutting. There is one saw which can be used to cut straight lines, circles, and curves and which can get into places where other saws simply can't reach. This is the turret saw—basically a pistol-grip-type handle which accepts a variety of blades. The usual turret saw is supplied with a blade for cutting wood and and a finer blade for cutting metal. With this saw, you can cut wood, composition board, metal fittings, copper tube, electrical cable, nails, and just about anything else that needs cutting in the average home.

Seldom do repair tasks in the home require extensive cutting, so it is best to get a small version of this saw. Get one which has a keyhole blade, a standard wood blade, and a blade for cutting metal.

The blades are usually held tightly with a simple locking jaw, and the turret can be positioned to cut in many directions. Whatever blade-holding system is used, make sure the blade is tightly locked and the turret secured before sawing.

Because the blades in these saws are light and tapered, sawing with the tip can result in twisting if too much pressure is applied at the handle. If you have heavy sawing to do—sawing which requires a fair amount of hand pressure—keep the sawing action up near the handle.

The blade of the turret saw can be locked in various positions. This can be especially handy when sawing near an obstruction, as when repairing shingles or siding outside.

Wall Scraper

The wall scraper is a tool which can be used to do a lot of things other than scrape walls. The tool experts may balk at some of the uses we propose for it but the fact that the scraper can be used to do many different jobs eliminates the need for at least two other tools.

The kind of wall scraper you should look for is made of tough steel and is fairly flexible. Test the flexibility of the blade, and buy the one which is stiff and springy. It should have about a 4-inch-wide blade.

The best scrapers are made of one piece of steel; that is, the shank of the handle is part of the blade. This shank is usually formed into a comfortable handle with two pieces of polished hardwood.

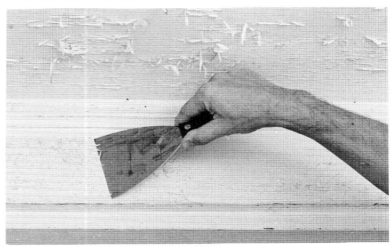

The wide scraper is handy not only for removing peeling paint, but for a wide variety of other jobs around the house.

The scraper will be used for scraping and also as a putty knife and for several other simple tasks. However, there is one job a scraper should never be made to do, and that is digging or using the blade as a chisel. The effectiveness of a scraper depends on a smooth edge and a flat surface. Because the best scrapers are made of carbon steel, there is often a problem of rust. By keeping the blade lightly oiled, you can prevent it from rusting.

Although it is difficult to break a scraper blade, it is possible to damage it when it is flexed too far. However, for the uses we will make of the scraper in this book, there should be no need for such pressure.

Monkey Wrench

There are almost as many types of wrenches as there are hammers. The monkey wrench isn't the easiest to use in tight places, but for the money spent, it will give you the biggest "bite" and broadest use of any of the adjustable wrenches. Get one that opens up to about 3 inches, but do not waste money on a heavy-duty model. Heavy-duty monkey wrenches usually have heavy handles and are as massive as pipe wrenches of the same size. The lighter version is not as heavy, but is more than adequate for every home repair job. This lighter version is often called an *auto wrench.*

As with the other tools, be sure to buy a top grade. Ask the hardware clerk for a wrench made of forged steel.

The jaws of a monkey wrench are flat, and care should be exercised to prevent nicking or gouging them. A nicked wrench face will score the surface of the work the wrench is being used on. Be sure to keep the adjustment spindle lightly oiled, and store the wrench away from sand and other gritty substances which could lodge in the threads.

Using a monkey wrench takes a little practice. Because the jaws are on the side of the handle, rather than on the end as with most other wrenches, the

The monkey wrench can handle many tightening jobs. Here the packing nut of a valve is being given a quarter turn to cure a leak around the stem.

workload will be off the centerline of the handle. However, if the wrench is snugged up tight enough to hold the work, but loose enough to allow removal for easy repositioning, you should have no trouble spinning large nuts.

The ordinary monkey wrench often has a rather long handle, and it takes relatively little pressure at the end to do a lot of work at the head. It's easy to damage a small tube or a bolt with only a small amout of pressure. When you're trying to loosen a "frozen" nut, valve, or other fixture, watch what is happening very carefully. Many times a few drops of penetrating oil on the threads a few minutes before the wrench is used will not only help loosen the nut, but also prevent the bolt from being sheared by the force of the wrench.

Never use a wrench for hammering. As rugged as a wrench may look, when you use it for work it wasn't designed for, you can nick it, break it, or damage the adjustment threads.

Plunger

This practical device is often called the "plumber's friend." But because it can solve so many home plumbing problems—without the plumber—it should really be called the householder's friend.

The plunger is used to loosen material clogging sink drains and toilets as well as minor obstructions in the main drain line. Essentially a home "first aid" device, it will not solve the big clogged-drain problems requiring the plumber. However, because most clogged drains are localized in sinks and toilets, this device is an indispensable part of your kit of tools.

There are a number of types available, ranging from the common cup-in-a-handle version to some rather elaborate units that look as though they came from the set of a science-fiction movie. While the common hemisphere model is probably as good as any

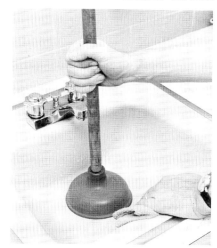

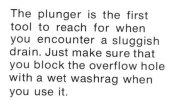

The plunger is the first tool to reach for when you encounter a sluggish drain. Just make sure that you block the overflow hole with a wet washrag when you use it.

other, the plungers with cones extended beyond the normal cup can exert greater force simply because of their greater internal capacity. But these more elaborate plungers are often designed only for use in a toilet.

The plunger is one tool to check occasionally. Because it is made of rubber or some synthetic material, it can dry out and become brittle. If not used for a long period of time, the plunger may fail when it is most needed.

The plunger is used to force water into the area of a pipe where an obstruction exists. Simply placing the plunger over the drain of a sink and pushing down on the handle will send a high-pressure ram of water at the obstruction. However, depending on the design of the sink or fixture, it may be necessary to do other things at the same time. Exactly what should be done in these cases will be described in detail in Chapter 10.

It should be remembered that the plunger can often cause future problems while eliminating present ones. When a sink trap is full of hair and is either completely clogged or running very slowly, it is always better to open the trap and remove the hair directly, rather than to use a plunger and possibly push the material further into the main drain line. A partially clogged drain line will only add to your problem.

These, then, are the seven simple tools we will be discussing. They should be on hand and ready for an emergency. Don't wait until the need is urgent to buy the tool you need. It's probably best either to buy a small toolbox or to find a special spot to keep the tools together. And, it's a good idea to keep this book with them.

Remember, buy the best tools. The cost is small, and the problems you can have with "bargain" tools just aren't worth the trouble.

Improvising Other Tools

Anything that does work can be considered a tool. Here are common household items that can be easily adapted as "tools."

Knife Whether it is a kitchen paring knife or a scout's pocket knife, this is an indispensable tool for many home repairs. No special kind is needed—only one with a good edge and a point.

Beer-can Opener Other than its prime task of providing a reward for a job well done, the common beer-can opener can be a very versatile tool.

Wooden Block Anything about 2 by 4 inches will do; its purpose is to hold sandpaper for a perfectly flat job. Many a parent has raided a child's construction set for just such a simple block.

Wire Coat Hanger Perfect for probing sink traps and toilets for drowned toys and bottle caps, wire coat hangers can also be bent into all kinds of shapes to do different jobs. They make great hooks for paint cans, clips for tools, stirring rods, and many other things.

Tape Measure   If you don't have a small pocket steel tape, you can always use a sewing tape or a school ruler.

Marking Materials   You will seldom need more than a well-sharpened pencil, but a piece of chalk can be very helpful when the mark must be removed.

General Household Supplies   These include such items as glue, transparent plastic tape, electrician's tape, oil, sandpaper, nails, tacks, screws, and other little things that tend to accumulate over the years.

It is surprising what can be done with seven basic tools and an accumulation of such "nontools" as we have just described. Most of the jobs tackled in the pages to follow will employ a combination of tools. Where the use is unusual—that is, unlike the conventional one—we will describe the procedure in detail.

In addition to using the tools safely, it is very important to store tools where they can cause no

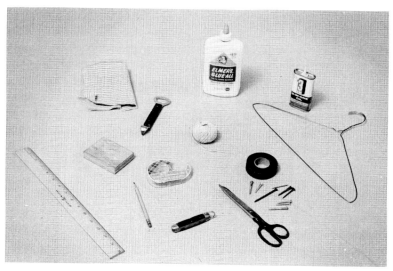

Any number of common household items can be improvised as tools to extend the usefulness of the seven basic tools.

harm to either children or adults. If you pick a kitchen drawer as your "toolbox," make sure everyone knows that it is for tools only. If your kit includes any chemicals which could be poisonous or flammable, store them in a remote, safe place.

Where special safety measures are necessary in the use of the seven simple tools, such as in electrical work and plumbing work, we will point out the precautions as we describe the individual jobs.

These are tools that can keep your house shipshape. Now, let's look at this house and how it is put together.

Chapter 2

HOW YOUR HOME IS PUT TOGETHER

WHY BOTHER?

THE SIMPLEST MAINTENANCE and repair jobs can be handled easily by following the instructions you will find throughout this book. So why should you know how your home is put together? After all, you don't need to know anything about the gasoline engine in order to drive a car. Why concern yourself with footings, flashings, studs, joists, rafters, and all those other strange-sounding parts of your home?

There is a good reason why a few minutes spent in studying "house anatomy" will be enormously useful to you in the future. Here it is: No single book could possibly cover all the various ills and faults that can befall a house or apartment and give you answers to each problem. We will touch on the more common problems; the uncommon ones have a habit of cropping up at 3 A.M. when repair shops don't answer phones.

By understanding the basics of your various house systems—or how it is put together—you'll surprise yourself with the ease with which you can diagnose and cure problems not even mentioned in these pages. In addition, you'll understand the reasoning behind the cures we do cover, and your self-confidence will grow enormously.

And, if you needed a clincher reason, here is one no one talks about—*householder's embarrassment.* Never more will you walk into a lumberyard or hardware store and feel that terrible flush of ignorance when you're asked how your joists are spaced or some other equally impossible-to-answer question. You will know.

FOUNDATIONS

Your house starts out as a big hole in the ground. If you build on the side of a mountain, or over a waterfall, or on some other out-of-the-ordinary location, then the hole might be dispensed with and piers or piles might be used to hold up your home.

The excavation looks like a mess, and usually is. But the builder knows how deep to scrape the hole, and the cumbersome excavating machines can do a good job of making the bottom of the hole relatively flat and level. The idea is to get down below the frost level and to find stable soil on which to start the foundation of the house. If the foundation isn't carried below the frost level, you'll risk all sorts of problems later on. As the ground freezes and thaws, it moves and heaves. If the foundation is in this area, it will heave, too, and will ultimately fail.

The first thing laid on the earth is a series of wooden forms about 16 inches apart that make a continuous trough in the outline of the house. The trough is filled with concrete; after the concrete has hardened, the wooden forms are removed.

This continuous ribbon of concrete about a foot thick is called the *footing* and is the place where all the weight of the house ultimately bears down on the soil. It is important that the soil be stable under the whole area of the footing. Unless you excavate down to solid rock and pour your footings on top of that, the weight of the house will cause the footings to settle slightly into the earth. The settlement will be relatively even and unnoticed if the soil is of the same character all over.

Problems are encountered when footings are laid over varying soils; one end may be poured on solid subsoil, while the other end might rest on spongy, organic material or soft, wet clay. Then the footing settles more at one end than the other and can cause serious problems later on. In extreme cases, houses have been known to split in two.

These details are not included to alarm you unduly. For the few people who have the opportunity to watch their homes built from scratch, we would advise you to snoop around carefully after the hole is excavated and before the footings are poured. If your home is a few years old, you have no need to worry. If it was going to split, it would have done so by now. If your home is only months old and a crack starts running down the foundation wall, keep a close watch on it. In virtually all cases, the crack is of no great concern structurally. But if it keeps getting wider, start hollering for the builder and the building inspector, the architect or engineer, and just about anyone else you can corner.

Foundation Walls

Today, most foundation walls are built of concrete or cinder blocks which rest on the footings. In some cases, the walls may be made of solid concrete which is poured in place in much the same fashion as the footings were. Older homes have a variety of materials in their foundations: brick, fieldstone, cut rock, etc. These masonry walls forming the cellar or base-

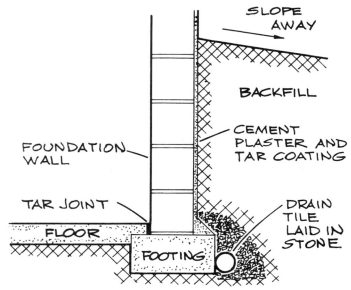

A typical foundation.

ment are carried up to a height between 7 and 8 feet.

Again, if you're having your home built, and you have some plans for finishing your basement, consider asking the builder to put another layer or "course" of blocks around the foundation. This adds another 8 inches to the height of your basement and immediately makes it a much more livable area.

The outside of the foundation must be carefully waterproofed if you want your basement to stay dry in every kind of weather. The last step in the mason's job is to apply a layer of cement plaster in one continuous coat over the whole foundation wall, from footing to top course. Over this a heavy layer of tar is painted.

If your basement has been consistently dry and then begins leaking even when you have no unusually rainy weather, it may be that the outside waterproofing has failed in some way. The tar eventually hardens, shrinks, and cracks; sometimes the cement plaster coat will develop cracks or loosen from the outside wall. While repairing such a problem is somewhat beyond your seven simple tools, it should be obvious to you how much work is involved and what a fair cost estimate should be from a professional. Such a condition is repaired by digging away the earth from the foundation wall, exposing all the faulty waterproofing, and then recementing and retarring the foundation wall or section that has failed.

Foundation Drains

The best way to keep water from collecting against your foundation wall, and eventually entering the basement, is to install foundation drains. The best time to do this is when the house is being built. The drains are nothing more complicated than perforated fiber pipe or short clay pipes called *tiles* that run around the foundation and eventually drain into a dry well or run off to a lower level in some fashion. The pipe is surrounded with stone so earth will not eventually fill in and clog the drains.

If your home was built without drain tiles and your water problem resists all other solutions, you might have to consider installing them after all. Installation is expensive at this stage because digging next to the foundation all the way down to the level of the footing is difficult with a machine; it has to be done by hand. If you ever do it yourself, you'll know what the Western Front was like with all that trenching.

Backfilling

You've got your foundation walls up and neatly plastered and tarred. Perhaps you've installed drain tile around the footings. At this stage, the building inspector will usually visit the site and check things out. So should you. If everything is OK, then permission is given to put all that dirt back against the foundation walls. This is called backfilling, and once it's done, you'll probably never see the outside of your foundation again. For this reason, it is wise to make sure all the waterproofing steps have been carried out properly before backfilling.

FRAMING

Framing is the name given to all the structural carpentry that starts from the top of your new foundation. Several systems are used, and they have such names as "Western," "platform," and "balloon" framing. The distinctions between them are important to young architectural students cramming for their exams; you needn't worry much about the differences.

Framing is really the wooden skeleton of the building. The outside is covered with a weather-resistant surface that you see, admire, and have to maintain. The inside is covered with various wall and ceiling treatments. It is important for you to know some of the general principles involved in framing a house, just as it is important for a doctor to know all about the skeleton that makes up the human body.

In both cases, the skeletons are hidden from view. And whatever you do on the outside has to be done with some regard for the skeleton underneath. For example, if you want to hang something heavy on a wall, it would be well if you could manage to hit part of that wooden skeleton, or framing member, and be sure your fastener lodges in solid wood instead of plaster that will crumble. But if you want a wire or pipe to pass through the wall, then you have to arrange some way of missing that framing member— or face a lot of drilling and possible damage to the member.

Joists and Sills

The first piece of wood laid on top of the foundation wall is called a *sill*. It is a large slab of wood, often

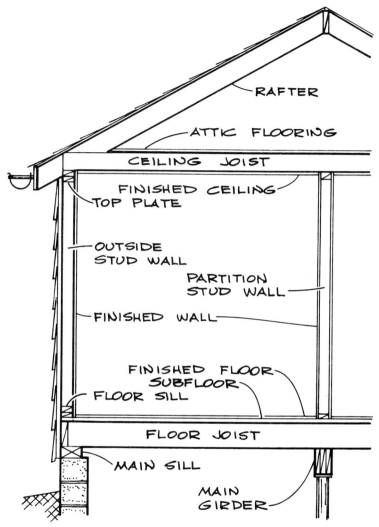

RAFTER

ATTIC FLOORING

CEILING JOIST

FINISHED CEILING
TOP PLATE

OUTSIDE
STUD WALL

PARTITION
STUD WALL

FINISHED WALL

FINISHED FLOOR
SUBFLOOR
FLOOR SILL

FLOOR JOIST

MAIN SILL

MAIN
GIRDER

Framing—the skeleton of a house.

made up of two pieces to give extra thickness, and is laid flat on the top course of the masonry wall. The sill usually rests on a bed of cement mortar which is slushed around it to fill gaps between wood and masonry. Every 10 feet or so, a large anchor bolt holds the sill tight against the foundation.

The sill is the first place you should look if you suspect termites in your house. These destructive pests will build mud tunnels inside or outside the foundation walls in order to get at that sill. And, once they've gotten into the sill, the rest of the wooden structure of the house is wide open to their appetite. If the foundation wall is built of hollow cinder block, the termites will often build tunnels inside the block and enter the sill unseen by any examination except one.

It's a good idea to get a long, sharp instrument like a knife, ice pick, or sharpened coat hanger. Poke around the sill, trying to stick the point of the tool into the wood. If termites have entered, no description of ours is necessary—you'll gasp at how easily the point penetrates affected wood members.

Sometimes a metal shield is laid directly under the sill on top of the foundation, and the ends are bent down on both sides of the foundation wall. This is an effective barrier to termite invasion (they can't build tunnels through or around the metal) and is appropriately called a *termite shield*. If you're building a house, ask the builder to install one and enjoy peace of mind for years to come.

The main beams are called *joists* and are usually spaced 16 inches apart. The ends rest on the sills on the outer part of the house and on a wood or metal beam called a *girder* in the center of the house. Joists which span a short distance are usually 6 inches in depth and get progressively larger in depth as the span increases. For larger spans, 10- and 12-inch depths are not uncommon.

You've probably experienced at some time a strange feeling that a floor is springy, or moving up and down as you walk upon it. The floor actually *is* moving up and down because the joists are not deep enough for the span. The only cure for such a condition is to add posts under the joists, in effect cutting the span in half.

If you look at your joists, you'll also notice little X-shaped constructions that tie all the joists together. These pieces of wood or metal are called bridging, and their purpose is to equalize the load among several joists instead of letting a single one take all the strain. Curiously enough, wooden bridging members can often be the cause of mysterious squeaks. As the joists move, the bridging members rub against each other and make an annoying noise. The cure is incredibly simple: Run a saw blade where the bridging rubs, and eliminate the rubbing and the squeaks with a quick stroke of the blade.

Subfloors

Subfloors are either planks or sheets of plywood that are laid on top of the joists and nailed securely along each joist. The subfloor provides a base for your finished floor, whether it be hardwood, tile, or whatever. The subfloor is also the chief cause of squeaky floors, so it is important that care be used in installing it. Once the subfloor is laid and squeaking tunefully, the only cure for the problem is from the underside. You have to get that subfloor tight against the joists by one or more methods which we'll discuss more fully later on.

Framing Walls

Inside and outside walls are constructed in basically the same way. A framework is built up of vertical pieces of wood called *studs* that are nailed to horizontal soles and plates. The *sole* is a piece of wood resting on the subfloor and spiked in place. The top plate holds the whole framework together. These framing members are also called "two-by-fours" because the nominal dimension of the wood is usually 2 by 4 inches. The lengths vary, of course, depending on how high or long the walls are to be.

Whenever you want to work on a wall—to hang a picture or shelf, install an electrical outlet, or what have you—keep the basic picture of vertical studs in mind. The standard distance between them is 16 inches, and you can find hints where the studs lie if you look carefully. And once you've found one, you can locate the rest by measuring 16 inches to the left or right.

One way to find a stud is to remember that electrical outlets are often nailed to one side or another of a vertical stud. Take off the cover plate and you'll see which side the stud lies on. Another way is to look for nails. If the walls are finished in material other than plaster, you'll be able to detect the nails or nail holes. The baseboard trim running along the bottom of the wall usually is nailed every 16 inches directly into a stud. Or, simply thump the wall with your fist and notice where you get a distinctive solid sound.

Finding the location of the studs is important in many cases. For example:

- Heavy shelves or mirrors are best fastened directly through the wall into a solid stud.
- Holes for electrical outlets must miss a stud because they are recessed in the space between the wall surfaces.
- Various types of wall panels are designed to be nailed every 16 inches into the studs.
- Openings for pipes, fixtures, wires, etc., are made much more easily if you know where the studs lie.

Extra studs are added around windows and other openings in the walls. In such cases, you have to use some care and common sense to discover the 16-inch pattern: the extra stud can easily throw off your measuring.

There's a hollow space about 3½ inches wide between the wall surfaces—the thickness of a two-by-four. Within this space a lot of stuff is crammed that you should be aware of. Water and drain lines run between the walls, as do electrical wires and gas pipes. Outside walls are also filled with some sort of insulating material, either as a loose granular fill or as blankets of mineral wool.

Again, a little common sense and some basement exploring will often tell you what lies between the walls upstairs. If you have to cut an opening in a wall that contains pipes or wires, use the saw slowly and carefully. It will take some carelessness on your part to cut a pipe or electrical cable. In old homes, however, an obsolete form of electrical wiring was often used that is no longer permitted. It was called *knob-and-tube work* and consisted simply of separate wires strung between insulating knobs or holders nailed to the walls. If knob-and-tube work exists in your house, always work with extreme care when cutting into a wall. Better yet, get rid of the unsafe system and update your electrical work according to the latest approved codes.

Ceilings

Resting on top of the plates are your ceiling beams or joists. If your home has two stories or more, the ceiling beams of the room below are the floor joists of the room above. There's usually little difference in spacing and size in such cases. If you have an unfinished attic or storage space, the ceiling joists are usually not quite as deep as regular floor joists for such a span.

This can cause a problem later on if you decide to finish off your attic with additional living space. The joists were not made to support such a load and will often cause cracks in ceilings below or give an uncomfortable springy sensation when you walk on the floor above. A cure is possible when you decide to finish that extra room—simply add extra joists up against each of the existing joists. This is called *doubling* the joists and will give you a solid floor for your expanded living space.

Rafters and Roof

Almost every roof slopes to some extent or comes to a pointed ridge. To hold up your roof at the proper angle, another set of beams are used called *rafters*. Rafters are spiked to the ceiling joists and the top plate of the outside walls. The roof rafters are covered with planks or plywood much like your subfloors. On top of this planking is laid the weatherproof roofing material—shingles, tiles, shakes, or slate. The edges of the roof carry rain gutters fastened to a fascia board which covers the ends of the rafters.

This now is your basic shelter. You have a weatherproof enclosure that keeps out wind, cold, and water. Now you have to make this shelter livable and comfortable. You need water, light, heat, and energy to run all your comfort systems.

UTILITIES

Water

Water is essential. It can come from water company mains or from a simple well dug in your yard, depending on where you live. However you get your water, it usually comes in at one point in the house and is then distributed to the various water-using systems. Later on, when we discuss plumbing, we'll go into detail on these various systems.

For the moment, keep in mind the skeleton of your house. Running up and down inside the walls are the veins and arteries of the home—the various hot- and cold-water pipes, and often pipes for heating. If you discover a strange leak someplace, you can usually trace your plumbing system from the source so that common sense will tell you where the problem is located.

Electricity

Electricity comes into your house from electric company mains at a place called the *main distribution panel*. Most people call it the *fuse box*, even when circuit breakers are used instead of fuses. The fuse box merely takes the main current coming in and breaks it down into smaller "pipes" or circuits which are distributed throughout the house. A modern house should have at least eight to twelve separate circuits. Each circuit is protected with a fuse or a circuit breaker in case you overload the circuit. If an overload does occur, having several separate circuits prevents undue inconvenience. The lights may go out in the dining room, but the stairs are still well lighted so you can go down into the basement and replace the fuse in safety.

Again, keep in mind the inside structure of your house skeleton; running all through your walls and floors are electric cables serving all parts of the house. Unlike pipes, which usually run in straight lines along joists, or at right angles to them, electric cables are typically arranged in random fashion. To keep lengths of wire at a minimum, all kinds of short-cut routes are taken to serve outlet boxes and switches. So when cutting into walls, be careful not to injure any part of the wiring. No hard-and-fast rules can be given about where you will discover an electric cable.

HEATING AND COOLING

There are several ways of heating your home. A furnace can warm air and then blow it through ducts to various parts of the house. Or the furnace can heat water and pipe it to various radiators in the form of hot water or steam. In some areas, electric heating elements are imbedded in walls, floors, or ceilings and heat the rooms by radiation.

Each of the systems has drawbacks and advantages, and we will not get into an argument about which is best. The question is academic at this point because you've got a system that you probably cannot change too easily even if you wanted to.

One thing to keep in mind: Regardless of your system, it is designed to provide a certain amount of heat. This heat is measured in British thermal units (Btu's for short) and is usually printed on a label attached to the furnace someplace. Your utility company or heating oil firm can tell you how many Btu's are needed to keep your house comfortable by taking into account the size of the rooms, amount of windows, degree of insulation, and the like.

If your house needs 180,000 Btu's and your furnace can deliver only 150,000 you will feel chilly at cold times of the year. Adding radiators or additional ducts will not cure the situation. You have either to cut down on the Btu's needed to heat your home by installing storm windows and doors and extra weatherstripping and insulation or replace your furnace with one of larger capacity.

WHAT YOU SHOULD KNOW
ABOUT BUILDING
MATERIALS

With your seven simple tools we don't expect you to attempt any new construction beyond installing a shelf or something equally simple. However, a little knowledge about the stuff your home is made of can be useful in your diagnosis of problems and help you find solutions for yourself. Let's go back to that big hole in the ground where your home starts.

Masonry

Any part of the house that touches the ground must be made of masonry or, in some cases, metal of some sort. The reason is simple—only masonry or metal can resist the action of rot, insects, and water. Masonry is a broad term and includes cement and concrete, brick and stone, and manufactured blocks made from various aggregates.

Concrete is a mixture of small stones, coarse gravel or sand, and portland cement. These ingredients are mixed together in the dry state; then a measured amount of water is added, and the mixture is finally poured or shoveled into forms for footings, walls, or walks. The proportions of stone, gravel, and cement are varied depending on the purpose of the final job. For the amateur mason, only a few things should be remembered:

- Concrete is figured by the cubic yard—that is, a volume of concrete that would completely fill a box 3 feet square on the bottom and 3 feet high. If you want a walk to be 4 inches thick, a cubic yard of concrete will cover 9 square yards (36 inches divided by 4 inches equals 9). If the walk is 3 feet wide, the cubic yard of concrete will cover 9 yards, or 27 feet, of walkway.

- Should you decide to build a concrete walk or a patio, you will save yourself a fantastic amount of labor if you buy transit-mix concrete. This comes in the familiar cement-mixer truck you see lumbering along roads with the gigantic barrel slowing turning in back. Once you've ordered a load of transit-mix concrete, there's no turning back. That truck looks more fearsome than a Sherman tank, and somehow you've got to shovel all that concrete into forms. Make sure you have lots of friends on hand!

- For smaller jobs, you can rent a small cement mixer where you buy the stone and gravel. These will mix 2 or 3 cubic feet of concrete at a time, so you can see how much work there is in mixing just 1 cubic yard. For most of the patching and repair jobs we cover in this book, a small sack of premixed concrete is the best choice. Actually, the small bags of concrete are really cement mixtures without larger stones. Premixed concrete is fine for small patch jobs, but hopelessly expensive if you have a fairly large hole you want to repair in a basement floor.

Cement is a mixture of coarser sand or gravel and portland cement. This is the mixture used for patching cracks and small holes and usually is what you get when you buy a small sack of patching mixture. A cement mixture is often used as a "topping" over concrete to make a smoother surface such as on a walk or patio.

Mortar is basically a sand cement with some added ingredients for workability. Mortar is used when laying bricks or blocks and should not set too fast, otherwise the mason would have difficulty in making adjustments to keep courses level and straight.

Cinder blocks, the masonry blocks often used in house foundations, come in a number of sizes, the most common one being about 8 by 8 by 16 inches. They are called cinder block because the main ingredients are cinders and fly ash obtained from furnaces used in various industrial processes. A cinder block is relatively light, fairly inexpensive, and perfectly adequate for typical house walls and foundations.

Because cinder blocks are relatively porous, it is important that outside waterproofing be done properly to prevent foundation leaks. On the other hand, you can drive special masonry nails into cinder-block walls almost as easily as you drive a nail into wood. This makes it easy to finish off basement areas: you can nail strips of wood to the masonry walls and then attach decorative wood panels or what have you.

Concrete blocks are similar to cinder blocks except that they are made from the same basic ingredients as regular concrete—coarse gravel, sand, and cement. They are heavier and more expensive than cinder blocks. Generally, these blocks are available in the same sizes as cinder blocks.

Brick and *stone* are being used less and less in home construction because of the expense. Any work you do with these materials will probably be simple repairs, such as replacing a loose brick. Bricks come in a variety of sizes and finishes for different purposes. Stone is usually limited to varieties of native stone in your area. The cost of shipping stone from a distance is enormous for the small amount of material compared to the weight.

Lumber

Basically, a lumberyard carries two broad types of lumber: framing lumber and finish lumber. You can easily guess the differences between the two. Framing lumber is the wood used to construct that skeleton of your home that we previously mentioned. It comes in a number of standard sizes and is used for joists, studs, plates, etc. Included with framing lumber are the rougher grades of plywood and planks that are used as a covering or sheathing of outside walls and the interior subfloors. Finish lumber is more expensive and shows in the cabinetry, trim, and paneling that finish off the inside and outside of the house.

Lumber sizes cause all kinds of confusion because the size you ask for is never the size you get. Any lumber calculations must take this fact into account, otherwise you'll find yourself with pieces that won't fit. The reason for this crazy system lies in the living nature of wood.

When harvested, timber is hauled to the mill in a green state and is cut to standard sizes based on the size of the log. A typical piece cut out of the log is a standard stud size that measures 2 by 4 inches by any number of feet in length, depending on the size of the log. That two-by-four is very rough from the mill saws and also has to be seasoned. As it is seasoned, the wood shrinks. Before it can be used, the surfaces have to be planed smooth by large machine planes. The end result is that the original piece of wood that measured 2 by 4 inches now measures 1½ by 3½ inches. But you still call it a two-by-four when you buy it, and you pay for 2 by 4 inches of lumber when figured on a board-foot measure.

In the Appendix we've included a table of lumber sizes that will help you buy the right size of lumber for any purpose.

Lumber Grades   Lumber grading can be confusing to the beginner and is usually the cause of a lot of unnecessary expense. The fundamental rule of buying lumber is this: *Buy the cheapest grade that will do the job adequately.*

Your lumberyard probably carries a single quality of framing lumber, which is usually a mix of two grades. The carpenter or builder who orders a load of framing lumber will pick out the best pieces for places where it is important that the wood framing be straight and sound. The pieces of lesser quality are used up where knots or straightness are not so important. Even if you're buying only a piece or two and taking it home sticking out the car window, try to pick out the lumber yourself.

Ordinary finish lumber—pine, redwood, and other woods used for shelves, furniture, and trim—comes in a number of grades. Most of the grading is done on the basis of appearance, that is, the number and size of defects showing in a given length. The most expensive piece of lumber you can buy is called *clear* and is just that. It is perfectly free from knots or other blemishes that would detract from its appearance. Use this grade *only* if you're interested in making your own furniture and want to stain it to show off the beauty of the wood. Nothing could be more wasteful than to buy this grade and then paint it.

Generally speaking, a typical lumberyard will carry another grade below clear called number 2 common. This grade has knots and blemishes that can be easily covered with paint or left natural as "knotty pine" if you're building a bookcase or a shelf. You'll be amazed at the saving when you buy this grade instead of clear for your projects.

Plywood   Plywood is graded by a system of letters and comes in two basic types: interior and exterior. The difference is in the glue that is used to hold the plywood together. Exterior plywood is made with waterproof glue and will resist prolonged weathering without peeling apart. Interior plywood will not hold up under such conditions of moisture, but is perfectly suited to interior construction in dry places. Needless to say, interior plywood is also less expensive than the exterior grade.

The two faces that show on a sheet of plywood are graded on appearance with letters, "A" indicating a first-grade surface, while "D" permits quite a few repairs, imperfections, and knotholes. Because most of the time only a single face shows, plywood usually comes with faces of two different grades on the same sheet—"A-D" is an example. The "A" face is used where it shows, while the imperfect "D" face is used as a back or surface that is never seen.

Roofing and Siding

A variety of materials are used to face the outside of the house and to make a watertight roof. There are different kinds of wood and aluminum siding, cedar and asbestos shingles, asphalt shingles, tiles, and slates for roofs, and much more. You won't, in the beginning, do much more than replace broken shingles or split siding. The best advice is to take the broken pieces to a building supply dealer or lumberyard and ask for a replacement.

Don't be surprised if you have to buy a bundle of composition or asphalt shingles when you need only a single strip. Also, it will be next to impossible to match colors since the shingles on the roof have been exposed for some time to the weathering action of sun and rain.

Nails and Fasteners

The building industry is one of the oldest, and it is understandable that much of its vocabulary should go back a long, long way. This is beautifully illustrated in the way a nail is identified. You ask for a "tenpenny" nail and you get a nail that is 3 inches long and is identified as "10-d" on the box or keg from which it comes. The "d" comes from the Latin *denarius*, which translates into "penny." In the old days, when nails were made by hand, you would get 100 nails approximately this length for 10 pennies. It follows, then, that if you wanted longer nails, they would use more metal and would cost more pennies. This is an easy way to remember that the higher the penny number of the nail, the longer the nail.

Better yet, when you're deciding on the size of nail you need, consult the chart we have included in the Appendix. You will also notice that nails come in a variety of styles and designs, each adapted for a special purpose.

For ordinary work you use what is called a *common nail*. A nail with a thinner body is called a *box nail* and is useful if you're nailing thin wood which would split if a common nail were used. For nailing trim and molding where you want inconspicuous nail holes, you use a *finishing nail*. This nail has a small head

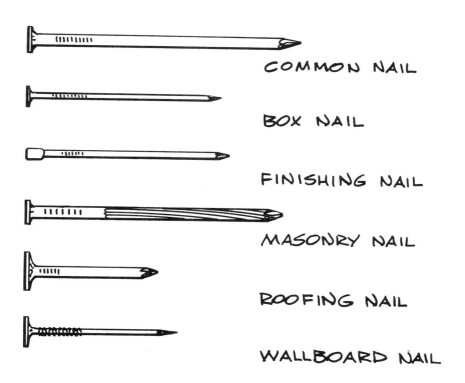

Different types of nails used in home construction.

which is readily countersunk with a nail set or simply by placing another nail on the head and lightly tapping it with your hammer. The small hole is later filled with putty or wood filler and painted over.

For outdoor work, you should consider using aluminum nails. These cost more than regular nails and are more apt to bend under a hammer blow. However, the trouble will be amply repaid in months to come. Ordinary steel nails quickly rust and streak siding and shingles with long lines of ugly rust stains. Aluminum nails keep your paint job clean for years.

Special nails are required for masonry; these are made of hardened steel and usually have a spiral design that offers more of a grip in the crumbly texture of the masonry.

Other special nails are available for specific jobs. Nails for asphalt shingles or roofing are made with large flat heads to prevent tearing of the roofing material. Nails for wallboards are usually heavily barbed on the shank to prevent the nails from popping and causing nailholes in wallboard walls. If you have any special fastening job, ask for advice from the dealer.

Other Fasteners A variety of special fasteners are available for special jobs. In addition, various types of adhesives are coming more and more into use. The day is probably not far off when nails will almost be eliminated in home construction and adhesives will take their place.

Interior Walls

Your interior walls can be made of a variety of materials. Most likely, they will be plaster or plasterboard covered with paint or wallpaper. Increasingly popular are panels of various sorts. These can be nailed or glued over existing walls when remodeling, or simply nailed to the upright studs in new work. Most of these panels have grooves suggesting planks, and although the grooves seem randomly placed, you'll always find two that are 16 inches apart—the standard distance between your studs. The finishing nail holding the panel is easily hidden in the groove.

In places where moisture is a problem, such as bathrooms, a common wall treatment is plastic or ceramic tile. These tiles are cemented to plasterboard walls in ordinary work. For quality work, the tiles are cemented on a cement-plastered wall. Such a wall will resist years of exposure to water with only occasional maintenance needed in replacing the fine cement between the tile joints.

The Rest of Your House

The basic materials used to build your home were just described. Even a small apartment will include many other elements that are necessary for everyday living. A home must have electrical and plumbing fixtures with all the necessary wiring and piping, hardware items like latches and locks, and an incredible variety of items that are more properly called decorative elements. Here would be included handrails, drapery rods, shelves, cabinets, special trim, and so on.

From time to time, repairs or replacements will have to be made. For most small jobs the simplest thing to do is to remove completely the defective part and take it to your local hardware or lumber dealer. Unless you happen to live in a very old place with obsolete hardware or other irreplaceable items, you can usually get an adequate substitute that will fit with little or no trouble.

Final Hints

This, then, is a brief look at the place you live in, including what you see and what you don't see behind the walls. We hope this picture will dispel much of the mystery of how your dwelling place is constructed; it was included to give you something essential—*self-confidence*. We trust, however, that we haven't gone too far on this score so that self-confidence turns to foolishness. Therefore, we urge you always to think twice when you reach for those tools.

Now—let's see what we can do to prevent a lot of problems before they even start.

Chapter 3

HOW TO STOP PROBLEMS BEFORE THEY START

NOWHERE IS PREVENTIVE maintenance more important than when you practice it around your living place. When you buy a new car, for the first few weeks you worry about every squeak and scratch. Then, as you accumulate mileage and dents, you probably let some preventive maintenance details go unattended, until finally you have only emergency repairs done. Then it's time for thinking about a new car.

Few people are in a position to let maintenance go unheeded in a home and then simply move into a spanking new home to start all over again. So it is important that you get into the habit of regularly checking your home, looking for potential warning signs of big trouble to come. By taking care of these small things now, a big repair bill can often be avoided later on.

If you're a neat, orderly person, you might even want to make some sort of checklist that you can refer to at regular times. Don't let us discourage you in this endeavor, but you can do a very good job if you just keep in mind the main systems of your house and mentally check them over whenever you're in the basement, attic, garage, or other part of the house. The main systems are the basic structural parts of the dwelling itself; the plumbing, heating, and electrical systems; and the *protective* systems. By this we simply mean the paint jobs that protect your house inside and out, the roofs and drains that keep you dry, and all the other surfaces which are exposed to wear and weather and which need regular renewal of one sort or another.

Which Comes First?

As you go through your home, certain jobs will require urgent attention, while others can be postponed for a more convenient time. Common sense will tell you which are small jobs for a rainy day. Our purpose here will be to point out jobs that should not be too long neglected. Later chapters will go into more detail about actual repairs.

If you live in an apartment, many of our suggestions will not concern you here because they are more properly the concern of the superintendent. However, you can make life easier for yourself (and the job easier for the super) if you spot troublespots before they become major problems. If you tell the owner about a damp spot on your ceiling, a needed repair can be made before the whole ceiling is ruined.

STRUCTURAL CHECKS

Again, here we are looking at the basic skeleton of the house, particularly where it shows in basements and attics. If your home is standing now, the chances are that it will be standing for a long time to come. Changes occur very slowly in the basic structure of the house, so an annual check is usually more than adequate. The following pages tell you what to look for.

Beams, Girders, and Joists

If the joists supporting the floor of a room are sagging, the problem is probably of long standing and you are aware of it by a number of signs. First of all, the joists or beams probably exhibit a slight sag as you look along them in the basement. Often, the floor resting on such joists is uneven and you notice that furniture is impossible to level. A cabinet may be flush against the wall at the floor, but stick out an inch or so at the top. In one extreme case we saw (in a house that went back to the American Revolution), a small piano would roll along the floor unless one side was wedged up. Such cases are rare, though.

Most of the time joists rest on two supports. One end of this floor beam is set on a wooden sill resting on top of the outside rim of the foundation, while the other end is set on a heavier beam that often runs down the middle of the basement. This heavy main beam is called the *main girder* and is made up of several pieces of heavy timber spiked together. Sometimes a masonry wall is substituted for the main girder. In any case, if joists are sagging, you certainly can't replace them.

The only way to fix this problem—and strangely enough it isn't as difficult as you may imagine—is to buy some special jack posts and slowly raise those sagging beams in the middle. Chapter 5 tells you how.

Wherever openings occur in the floor, such as for a stairway, the joists are prevented from resting on the foundation sill. There are a number of ways carpenters solve this problem, the most common being to install a short beam at right angles to the joists called a *header joist*. Header joists are notched and rest on strips of wood nailed along the bottom edge of the main joists. These strips are called *ledger strips* (because they form little ledges). Sometimes ledger strips begin to pull loose from the weight of the header joist. Some long nails and a sturdy hammer arm will quickly put these ledger strips back tight and prevent serious sag problems later on.

While you're in the basement looking up, examine those X-shaped constructions between the joists called *bridging members*. Sometimes these work loose and should be nailed up tight again. If they touch in the middle, work the blade of your turret saw through the space and eliminate possible future squeaks.

Dampness and Mildew

The basement is probably the first place you notice dampness and mildew. Often, these problems are tolerated for long periods of time even though the cure would be simple. Chapter 5 will tell you how to tell the difference between the various dampness and water problems and the specific solutions for each.

It's a good idea to take a quick trip down into the basement whenever it's raining very hard. You can shut that open window which is letting the rain in. More important, if you have a leak, you can usually find out where it is coming from while the rain is in progress. It's tough to trace the sources of a puddle hours after the rain has stopped.

Often, outside causes of wetness can be solved very easily. Puddles rest against the house and cause dampness in the basement when a little raking will eliminate the puddle completely. Cutting back on overgrown shrubs will keep wet leaves from ruining an exterior paint job. Cleaning out window wells around cellar windows will go a long way toward making the basement feel and smell less murky.

Dry Rot and Termites

Every piece of wood within a few inches of the ground should be looked at carefully. All sorts of rot and decay can start if a piece of wood, such as a door sill, is

Short beams called *header joists* are notched on the bottom and rest on strips of wood called *ledger strips.* If the ledger strips look loose, nail them back in place with some heavy nails.

constantly exposed to the action of moisture and insects near the ground.

Termites are a big problem even when you think the wood members are safe. These creatures can build intricate tunnels of mud, sometimes several feet in length, just to get at a piece of your house. Every inch of your foundation should be regularly examined for these tunnels, inside and out. In particular, look around openings in your foundation where pipes or wires enter because this makes their job of entry that much easier. And don't think the opening is too small for these pests. If you can stick a knifeblade in the crack, that's all the room they need. More about them in Chapter 5.

Exterior woodwork and structural members should be examined at the same time. Posts, porches, trellises, and the like are all subject to the same kind of damage.

OUTSIDE CHECKS

The exterior of your house is subjected to severe wear by wind, sun, rain, snow, and other forces. If your property is blessed with trees, then you have an additional problem when leaves rain down on your house, clogging gutters and drains.

Surfaces that are more or less horizontal are the first to show wear and should be checked. This would include door- and windowsills, porch floors, canopies and trellises, and gutters. Most of the time, simple scraping of loose paint and touch-up painting are all that is needed.

Gutters are a different matter. If they are wood, then you have to face up to a yearly job of oiling the insides of the troughs. A gallon of linseed oil and a dishmop are all you need to keep the wood from drying out and cracking. Once cracks develop and go through the wood, you will face an expensive replacement problem. It's a messy job working on ladders and roofs, but it should be done if you want to prevent a bigger job later on.

Metal gutters need less maintenance than wood, a simple cleaning out of leaves and plant debris usually being sufficient. If the gutter is long and joined with a sheet-metal fitting someplace near the middle, then check that fitting. It is made waterproof with a sealant of some sort. After a while the sealer will dry out and the joint will leak. If the sealer looks dry, scrape as much of it off as you can and then apply a fresh coat. Sealers come in various types and are readily available in hardware stores under different brand names in easy-to-use squeeze tubes.

While you're wearing your sneakers and walking on the roof, don't forget to look at the chimney and the way it is waterproofed where it meets the roof line of the house.

Chimneys and ventpipes are waterproofed with

pieces of sheet metal called *flashing* that is made weathertight with a black, tarry roof compound. Flashing is also used where two roof lines join, making a valley down which the rain drains. It will be obvious to you if these need attention. The tar gets brittle after a few years. Replace it with fresh compound, which you can apply with a short, flat stick.

It's unlikely you can find a roof leak by looking from the outside. Rather, look around the inside of the roof in attics and crawl spaces. Sometimes you can spot a roof leak before it gets bad enough to let you know downstairs on the ceiling; look carefully for small leaks that have caused water stains on roofing boards or insulation.

Also, if you discover a stain line, you can often follow it back to where the actual leak is occurring. If you do discover a roof leak by means of a wet spot on your ceiling, you'll seldom find the actual leak directly above that spot. Most likely, the water is leaking in and running along a beam for a distance before it finally decides to give you notice.

Another source of weather damage is where two different materials are joined on the outside, such as the joint between bricks and shingles above, between window or door frames and the siding of the house, and in similar locations. These joints are made waterproof by means of caulking, which is a puttylike substance forced into the cracks with a caulking gun.

When you have your house repainted, insist that the painter recaulk all exposed joints. If the caulking dries out between paint jobs, you can touch it up with caulking compound from a convenient squeeze tube.

Windows

While you're still outside making your preventive maintenance checks, make sure you examine all your windows, looking particularly for loose putty. Usually, your window putty will last from one paint job to the next. If it should dry out and fall away from the glass, replace it with fresh putty or glazing compound. You can buy a small can in a paint store and use your scraper as a reasonably good putty knife to make a good-as-new repair.

To make sure the repair will last, you should coat the window frame with a layer of paint or linseed oil before applying the putty. Raw, dry wood quickly absorbs the linseed oil out of the putty and causes it to fail again if you don't take this precaution.

Roofs and Sidings

These are lumped together here because your maintenance problems are similar. In either case, you may discover a shingle that is cracked or missing. Where do you buy a single shingle? You can't. There are two ways of solving this problem.

The first is to buy a bundle of shingles, either strip shingles for your roof or cedar shakes for the side of your house. Actually, a whole bundle in either case isn't fantastically expensive, except that it seems so wasteful to buy a bundle when you need only one to do the job.

The other way is to become a scrounger. If some new homes are being built in your area, you can almost always find scraps being thrown away by the builder that you can use for repair jobs. If you see a model home going up while on a Sunday drive in the country, don't be afraid to stop, look around, take a brochure from the salesperson, and pick up a scrap shingle or two on your way back to the car.

If your house siding consists of long boards, one or two of which have begun to split, replacement is easier. Lumberyards will sell you only as much as you need. The same is true of bricks; you can buy as few as you want.

If your siding is aluminum that sports a dent from

a baseball, the only thing we can advise is to call in a professional and be prepared to weep. This is not a repair job for you and your simple tools.

INSIDE CHECKS

It's amazing how much more pleasant your everyday living can become if you just walk through the house some day with a screwdriver in your pocket. Everything that moves, turns, hinges, rolls, or what have you has a piece of hardware someplace. And this hardware is probably held in place with screws that could stand some tightening.

Therefore, we suggest an important maintenance job is simply tightening all those screws. Hinges on doors and cabinets, strike plates, locks on windows and doors, handrails—these and many other items all should get your once-over.

At the same time, it would be a good idea to carry a small can of oil during this chore because most of the

Go through your home with a screwdriver and an oilcan, and you will make life a lot more pleasant.

items that need tightening could also use a drop or two of lubrication to make operation easier.

Walls and ceilings should be examined for several signs that could mean more serious trouble later on. The first are signs of dampness indicating leaks from weather or pipes inside the walls. If walls are covered with wallpaper, dampness may not be apparent as a stain, but the paper will probably be starting to loosen.

The second most common fault is cracks in plaster. Akin to plaster cracks are the small round holes produced by nails that pop in plasterboard walls. An easy way to mark these places so you won't miss any when you start repairing them is to use a piece of chalk. The chalk marks also nag you into getting the job over with as fast as possible.

While you're walking around looking at walls and ceilings, you'll probably discover squeaks in floorboards here and there. Remember where these occur because the only way you'll be able to fix such annoying noises is by getting at the floorboards from the underside.

Floors get a lot of wear, particularly near doors or other passageways. In Chapter 6 we'll tell you how to fix various kinds of floors. However, you can prevent a lot of problems by remembering that the two greatest enemies of floors are water and dirt. Water will ruin the finish on wood floors, stain the wood, and make complete professional refinishing inevitable. Hard dirt, particularly gritty dirt brought in from outside, will also quickly ruin the finish on wood and composition floors. No amount of waxing can prevent such damage because it is caused by abrasion.

Make sure you have mats outside the doors so the worst dirt will come off shoes before they enter the house. Regular sweeping, even if only in the entrance area, can do a lot to preserve the new appearance of floors and floor coverings throughout your home.

Stairs should get your attention at this time, also. Anything that could cause accidents should be cleared up as soon as possible. Tack down loose floor coverings in front of stairs. Make certain that the stairs are free from loose treads or tread coverings, that runners are not loose, and that all handrails are tight. Stairs cause most of the accidents around the home, so anything you can do to improve safety here will prevent grief later on.

Finally, do you have fire extinguishers in places like the kitchen, furnace room, workshop, and laundry? Most important: *When was the last time you tested them?*

PLUMBING CHECKS

Most people never bother to look at their plumbing system until a leak or a strange wet spot tells them something is amiss. This is too bad; a few minutes spent each month looking for trouble signs can often prevent costly damage later on. We would urge you to use the following suggestions as a checklist. Later on, as you become more knowledgeable, you will almost automatically spot potential problems as you use basins and sinks, do the laundry, water the lawn, or perform any of a dozen chores requiring the use of water in some way.

Emergency Treatment of Leaks

Everyone living in your home should know where the main shutoff valve is *and* how to use it. You'll find the main valve right next to the water meter where the main water line comes into your home. In a panic situation it is often quite easy to forget that a valve is closed by turning the handle in a *clockwise* direction. You might want to paint this instruction near the valve. It's also a good idea to occasionally close and open the valve to make sure slow corrosion or the

Shutoff valves are placed on each side of your water meter. Either one can be used to cut off the flow of water throughout the house.

accumulation of minerals does not cause the valve to jam in an open position.

Banging Water Pipes and Other Frightening Noises

Most plumbing problems mature in silence until one day—*pop*—and a leak starts from a water heater, a pipe joint opens, or some other heretofore unnoticed problem clamors for attention. Not so with the phenomenon called *water hammer.*

Water hammer is just that—a hammering of a column of water on all the pipes in your house. You'll notice water hammer if your water pressure is high and you close a faucet sharply. That hard, rapping sound that reverberates throughout the piping system is water hammer. The quick-acting electrically operated water valves on washing machines and dishwashers will commonly cause water hammer.

Especially dangerous is the kind of water hammer

that starts to resonate and grow in intensity. Usually this happens when you're using the bathroom and you shut off a faucet at the same time the toilet tank is filling up after being flushed. In this set of circumstances, the float in the toilet tank may begin vibrating, rapidly opening and closing the water valve in the tank. In such a case run to the faucet—any faucet in the house—and open it quickly. This will dissipate the vibrating energy and prevent serious damage to your plumbing system. Then close the faucet slowly.

Other types of water hammer are caused by long, unsupported lengths of piping. These pipes should be supported as described in Chapter 10, which covers plumbing repairs in detail. This is about the only type of water-hammer problem that the amateur can handle. The other problems described above require the installation of a pressure-reducing valve or a *relief column* by a professional plumber.

Running Toilets

There is absolutely no reason why you should tolerate a toilet that hisses forever after it is flushed or is continually wasting water by not shutting off completely. Later on we'll show you how to fix a variety of such problems like an expert.

Here we would impress you with the idea that you should take prompt steps whenever it seems the flushing mechanism is not working properly. Too often, people think that something is wearing out and repairs or replacement will be time-consuming and expensive. And they go on living with a condition that could be cured as simply as bending a wire or wiping off some grit from the rim of a stopper.

Leaks and Strange Wet Spots

Eventually, a leaky pipe will announce itself with a damp spot on wall or ceiling, a puddle, or even a flood. Good sense says you should try to spot a potential

Mineral deposits and corrosion around the packing nut of a valve mean trouble. Replacing the packing is a simple job.

leak before it causes damage far out of proportion to the size of the repair.

You can't predict when and where a pipe will burst (which is quite rare apart from freezing damage), but you can usually spot joints that will cause you trouble. Look at where the pipes are joined together mechanically with elbows, unions, or the like. If you see some discoloration or mineral deposits, or even a collection of granular material around the joint, watch out. You probably have a slow leak which will only get worse in time.

Look at faucets, particularly around the stem of shutoff valves that are installed on hot and cold lines serving various fixtures throughout the house. A very common source of slow leaks is around the washing machine. The shutoff valves to which the hoses are connected are often a nuisance to turn off. And if they haven't been turned for a while, it can take a bit of muscle to shut off the water completely. The result is inevitable: As the rubber hoses age, they get weaker until one day they burst—usually when you're away from home.

Get in the habit of turning off the water valves after you've used the washing machine. If that's too much trouble, have a plumber install a special single-lever valve that is especially designed to serve washing machines. One twist of the wrist and both hot and cold water lines are turned either on or off.

Other Common Problems

Other problems with your plumbing system that are obvious from the start are slow-running drains and noisy pipes other than those resulting from water hammer. Often, it's merely a loose or worn washer in the faucet that causes all the squeals. These problems are too easy to fix to tolerate the nuisance. You won't need any sort of checklist to spot them; every time you run water you'll be reminded of them and the fact that they are fairly easy to cure, as described in Chapter 10.

Prevent Trouble Before It Starts

A frozen pipe can cause incredible damage. Your plumbing check should try to spot potential freeze-ups. Usually, a pipe will freeze if it's in an open space fairly unprotected from the weather. Water pipes that go up outer walls that are not insulated and pipes in a garage that is open to cold weather are particularly susceptible to such damage.

Insulate wall areas to keep pipes from freezing. Sometime insulating the pipe will help; you can quickly install insulation that comes in the form of split tubes or thick tape. In extreme cases, you can install electric heating cable that will warm the pipe above the freezing level whenever the temperature drops below a certain point.

No plumbing check would be complete without

checking the condition of the main drains in your home. Such catch basins may be in your basement, in the garage, or even on your driveway. It's a messy job, but you should take the cover off regularly and remove debris that will only clog the drain and make cleaning even messier later on.

HEATING SYSTEM CHECKS

Most heating systems are very reliable and efficient, provided they receive some minimum maintenance and attention. The kind of checks depends on the kind of heating system you have in your home.

The first thing to get straight is the difference between the type of fuel you use to heat your house and the type of system that actually warms you. The principal fuels are oil, gas, coal, and electricity. Any of these fuels can provide the energy for different types of heating systems—radiant, hot-water, hot-air, or steam.

Energy Sources

First about fuels. Gas and electricity are supplied by utility companies, and safe delivery to your home is their responsibility. Don't try to repair anything yourself. Call the utility company at once if you smell gas or suspect an electrical hazard. The only thing you should do is turn off the main valve (near the gas meter) or the main switch on the electric meter.

An oil tank is either in your basement or buried in the ground outside. Interior tanks are good for many years, and the only thing you should look for is small leaks around pipe joints.

Outside tanks will sometimes corrode and leak away your supply of oil, all unknown to you until you discover your tank is empty at the start of the heating season. You can keep an eye on this situation

quite simply. At the end of the heating season, when you're sure no more oil is going to be used until the following autumn, measure your oil supply. Use a stick and mark the level accurately. After a couple of months, measure your supply again. Any noticeable change in level probably means a leak in the tank.

Coal, of course, needs no attention unless you have an automatic stoker attached to your furnace. Foreign objects, such as odd bits of scrap metal in the coal, can jam the feeding mechanism. The solution is obvious—make sure you don't use the coalbin as a dumping area for any kind of scrap.

Heating Systems

Now about different heating systems. *Radiant systems* heat with invisible rays emanating from the source of heat. Modern electric heat, where wires are embedded in ceilings, are pure radiant systems. So, too, is the old-fashioned wood-burning stove that radiates heat from the hot metal. There are no moving parts, so maintenance is negligible.

Hot-water systems use a furnace to heat water somewhat below the boiling point and then circulate the hot water throughout the house by means of pipes and radiators. A modern hot-water heating system can be very efficient and stingy as far as space requirements go. It is entirely possible to heat a fairly large house with a furnace that can fit easily inside a small closet. By means of electrically operated valves connected to room thermostats, it is also possible to "zone" the system so that heat is delivered only to rooms calling for heat and bypassing warm rooms entirely.

Steam systems also use water, but the furnace must heat the water above the boiling point so that steam is formed. Steam pressure forces the hot steam to radiators all over the house. After a while, the steam cools inside the radiators and condenses into water. The radiators and connecting pipes permit the water to flow by gravity back down to the furnace and boiler to be heated into steam again.

A hot-water or steam radiator gets warm and radiates heat. It also is shaped so that air is drawn in at the bottom, warmed by contact against the warm metal, and then distributed at the top by convection air currents to warm the room.

The most efficient hot-water or steam radiator is the kind that stands naked and ugly in a room. Radiator covers, while they make sense as decoration, will inevitably cut down both radiant and convective heat. If your color scheme can possibly stand it, try to paint radiators black. If you have a metal grill hiding the radiator, paint that black too. Black is efficient in radiating heat. Light colors, particularly gold and silver paints, act as insulators and keep heat from leaving the radiator.

Some hot-water heating systems use radiators in the form of baseboards that run along one or more sides of a room. The efficiency of these can be seriously reduced if you let dust accumulate on the inside. Simple maintenance here is merely to run the vacuum cleaner over the fins regularly. Neither should you let drapes cover them and interfere with the flow of air.

Convection or hot-air systems are very simple. Air is warmed in a furnace and forced through ducts throughout the house. In old-fashioned systems, the warmed air rose naturally through a large grill in the floor and circulated more or less naturally through the rooms. Modern systems use smaller ducts and a fan to force the air to remote rooms. Anything that will impede the flow of air will impede the heating system. Therefore, make sure that large pieces of furniture or heavy drapes do not cover hot-air openings or registers.

Maintenance of Your Heating System

Now that you have some idea how you stay warm in winter, maintaining your heating plant should become less mysterious. Most of the time, efficient maintenance means not much more than regular cleaning of the system. It is natural for a heating system, which circulates large amounts of warm air, to accumulate a lot of dirt and dust which will impair its heating capacity. Therefore, make it a regular part of your spring and fall cleaning chores to run a vacuum hose all around inside radiators and grills, on fins and other types of heat exchangers in your rooms, and even around the furnace. Filters should be replaced according to the instructions on the furnace. A clogged warm-air filter can cost you a lot more than the price of a new filter, so it is poor economy to stretch filter life.

Hot-air systems have fans run by electric motors; hot-water systems usually have pumps run by motors, too. In each case, you'll find labels or instructions fastened nearby that tell you where and how often to oil moving parts.

Hot-water systems have another peculiarity which should be checked. Air is dissolved in the water circulating throughout the system and eventually forms pockets in radiators where no hot water reaches. In such a case, the radiator is only radiating a portion of the heat it is designed to provide and you will notice the room feels cooler. Instead of setting up the thermostat, which merely makes the pump and motor run longer and harder, you should "bleed" the radiator. Near the top you will find a little valve which is opened with a small key. Open the valve slightly and you'll hear a hiss. When the hiss stops and you see a drop of water form on the valve, you know the radiator is properly filled with water. Do this on every radiator in the house, once or twice a heating season.

Steam radiators also have valves that permit air to be forced out of the radiator during the warming cycle, but keep the steam inside. These little valves should be considered expendable items; once they get noisy and leak steam, replace them completely. This will take a minute or two with your pliers.

Steam systems, because they depend on gravity to return condensed water back to the boiler, are also susceptible to seemingly major problems. Some radiators will never get warm, and pipes will bang and knock to an alarming degree. Both these problems can be traced to the return water collecting somewhere along the line and acting much like a trap in the plumbing system. Steam will not pass the water trap to heat certain radiators. Steam pressure will also force the column of water up and down the piping system with resulting noises.

Find out where the water is collecting and most of your problem is solved. You have to eliminate the trap action of the pipe by making water flow by gravity. Usually a pipe has slipped so that water cannot flow uphill back down to the boiler. If you tilt or wedge the pipe or radiator to establish a normal gravity flow, you're home free.

Remember, also, that many of the problems of a hot-water or steam system are similar to typical plumbing problems. Water and piping are involved in each. Therefore, look for pipe joints that might be leaking, unsupported lengths of piping that may be vibrating, and valves that drip. With only a small investment in time, you can be relatively sure that you will stay warm and comfortable throughout the winter and not run into unforeseen problems.

ELECTRICAL CHECKS

No program of home maintenance is complete without thorough electrical checkups. You might wonder why your electrical system, with few moving parts to get out of order, should be examined several times a year. The answer is simple:

When installed originally, your electrical system was probably adequate for the needs of the day. With the passage of years, you have undoubtedly bought extra appliances and have otherwise added to the load the system was designed to carry. Sometimes these additions are very makeshift and hazardous, as when you snake extension cords under rugs because you haven't enough wall outlets to serve all your needs.

For safety's sake you should not permit unsafe conditions to persist, especially when you can probably do a lot of the work yourself with your few tools.

Signs of an Overloaded System

If you blow fuses or circuit breakers frequently, notice a dimming of lights when certain appliances are turned on, or see your TV picture get smaller when a switch is thrown, you can be fairly certain your wiring is overloaded. Sometimes the overload is in a single circuit and the cure is simply to take some appliances off the overloaded circuit and plug them into another circuit serving other outlets. Chapter 11 on handling electrical repairs will show you how to map the various circuits in your home and how to figure the safe load each can carry.

On the other hand, if all the circuits in your house are working near their limit, you should waste no time in calling in a professional to add extra capacity to your electrical system.

Unsafe Extensions

Extension cords are among the worst offenders against electrical safety because most people misuse them or don't understand their true purpose. An extension cord is perfectly acceptable as a very temporary means of getting power to an area not regularly served by an outlet. The important thing to remember in using it is that it *is* temporary. When the task is done, disconnect the extension cord and put it away.

Problems arise when people use extension cords as permanent parts of their electrical systems. Lamps, fans, heaters, and a host of applainces are indiscriminately plugged into the extension cord. And to make matters worse, the extension cord will often be buried under the rug or snaked behind furniture where furniture legs can rub against the wire and abrade the insulation.

Step 1 in your program of electrical safety is to remove all those unsafe extensions; the risk is not worth the price of having extra outlets added where you need them.

Akin to the extension-cord danger is the "octopus" wiring risk. You've seen an electrical octopus—it's a regular outlet that is loaded beyond it's capacity. One or more three-way plugs are used to extend the num-

The first step in any house inspection is to get rid of unsafe extensions.

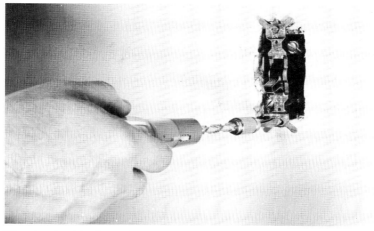

Simple electrical repairs are well within your capability.

ber of appliances that the solitary outlet has to serve. The resulting picture looks like an octopus with all those separate wires coming from a single source.

At the same time you're picking up extension cords, you should unplug all those overloaded outlets. Again, this is a sign your electrical system is inadequate and needs the immediate attention of a professional.

Switches and Outlets

Next, you should test all your switches and outlets to make sure they work. Repairing these is well within your capabilities, and there's no reason why you should have outlets that don't function.

Switches will go after a while because the constant on-off operation will eventually wear out the snap springs inside the switch. When the time comes to replace them, you should consider the somewhat more expensive mercury or silent switches that are both silent and longer-lasting.

Outlets generally go "dead" not because of mechanical difficulties, but because some careless painter has allowed paint to get inside the outlet and act as an insulation on the contacts. Rather than try to clean off the paint, you should replace the entire outlet with a new receptacle. Again, this is an easy job needing nothing more than a screwdriver and your pliers.

Doorbells should be considered here because the problem of repair is similar to those above. A doorbell push button is a very simple switch that works on low voltage. Because it is often exposed to the weather, it is not uncommon for the switch to accumulate dirt or a coating of oxide on the contacts. Result—no current passes and the doorbell is dead. Replace the switch; it is so inexpensive that it usually isn't worth trying to disassemble the old one to clean the contacts.

Permanent Fixtures

Permanent fixtures include such things as lighting units, fans, heaters, and similar installations. Apart from the electrical connections, which are similar for all kinds of fixtures, there are a number of mechanical things that can cause problems. Usually, you'll find that a fastening screw is loose or missing. A minute or two with screwdriver and pliers are all that is needed to make sure a petty annoyance doesn't eventually turn into a major repair job.

Upgrading Your Electrical System

Next time you're in a large electrical store, take a look at the various fixtures, appliances, and repair parts available. An inadequate kitchen light can be easily replaced with a modern, glare-free fixture that will flood every corner with light. Undercounter fluorescent fixtures make food preparation much easier, while a dimmer switch in your dining room will make entertaining much more spectacular.

Dozens more examples could be cited. The point we

want to make is that most of these improvements that upgrade your electrical system are not at all difficult to install. In fact, most of the time you merely replace an old fixture with a new one without any additional complicated wiring or mechanical operations.

So, whenever you're faced with a repair or replacement task, explore the alternatives available. You'll find that your reputation as a fix-it genius will be assured among your family and friends.

SPECIAL SEASONAL CHECKS

We've discussed the most obvious jobs you should attend to in your plan of preventive maintenance, and most will probably be taken care of more or less casually as conditions make themselves known. However, there are certain things you should attend to on a regular, seasonal basis. It makes sense, for exam-

A push button for your bell or chimes is replaced merely by connecting two wires to the screws in back of the button.

ple, to check your roof before the storms of winter arrive. You certainly don't want to walk on an icy roof, in freezing weather, to fix a leak that could have been handled much more easily on a nice fall day.

Spring and fall are the two seasons of the year you will discover as providing most of your regular chores. The reason is simple: After the brunt of winter, there are a lot of repairs to be made, in addition to preparations for summer. And in the fall, you should get ready to face the winter with everything sound and in working order.

Here, then, are jobs you should consider by season:

Spring

1. The first thing to do is to inspect the house for winter damage and make a list of repairs that should be done. Arrange the items in order of importance. Fix a damaged roof before you fix a hole in the driveway, for example.

2. Pick the first warm day available to fix damaged roof shingles.

3. While you're on the roof, attend to any repairs around the chimney or in the flashing around roof openings.

4. Clean and repair gutters. If they're wood, use the linseed oil treatment we previously mentioned. At the same time, examine and clean the leaf guards over the openings into the downspouts. Make sure your downspouts are all open and clear so spring rains will be carried off the roof quickly.

5. If the cold weather has made caulking brittle, scrape off the dried pieces with a can opener and apply fresh caulking compound from a tube. If it appears caulking will be a big job, it's probably time to consider getting your house painted, since caulking and paint wear at about the same rate. If you want to handle a

big caulking job yourself, consider renting a caulking gun at the paint store.

6. If no major paint job is planned, you still will need touch-ups on areas that wear particularly fast—like doorsills, porch floors, outside doors, and trim exposed to unusual wear.

7. Masonry often needs attention after freezing weather. Repair small cracks in walls, walks, and foundations. Pay attention to joints between bricks, repairing the mortar joints as needed.

8. If you have separate screens and storm windows, make the switch now. If storm windows need repair or paint, do it before storing them away for the summer. When winter comes you'll marvel at your foresight and good sense because you'll be in no mood to repair them when the weather has suddenly turned cold.

9. Clean and inspect your furnace for needed repairs once cold weather has passed. If you have a service contract, call the service company or utility now. You'll be amazed at what fast service you can get on furnace repairs during warm weather. If you wait till fall, you may discover a waiting list a mile long.

10. Look over any trees you may have on your property. Winter may have weakened some limbs, so now is the time to consider calling in a tree man to trim and protect your trees.

11. Finally, a good general spring cleaning, inside and out, is usually needed to complete your spring maintenance chores and to make you look forward to a fairly worry-free summer.

Summer

1. Summer is pretty much an off-season as far as repairs go, unless of course you let needed spring tasks slide until now. If so, get them

done before the weather gets so hot you won't be in the mood for outdoor work.

2. Summer is a good time to take notice of insect damage or potential damage from various kinds of pests. Call in a professional exterminator if you suspect termites, discover little piles of fine sawdust produced by carpenter ants, or see damage from other destructive insects that may be attacking your home.

3. Do any outside jobs that will make for fewer problems in the fall and winter. Trim branches that rub against walls or gutters, rake out low spots near foundation walls to prevent puddles from forming, reset flagstones along walkways, and so on.

4. Warm, humid weather will usually swell doors and windows, making them difficult to operate. This is a good time to make such repairs.

Fall

1. Fall is the time to prepare for winter, so try to spot potential problems in a thorough inspection. A small repair now can prevent a lot of trouble during the middle of winter.

2. Take down separate screens (if you have them), and repair and paint them before storing for the winter. Comes spring, you'll be glad you did this job early.

3. If you haven't checked your furnace, don't delay any longer. This is the busy season for heating companies, and the later it gets, the longer it takes to get service. Replace hot-air filters.

4. After the leaves have all fallen, clean out your gutters and roof drains to prevent moisture and frost damage later on.

5. Check all places for potential cold-air leaks once

the wind starts howling. Repair or replace weatherstripping around doors and windows, make sure caulking is tight and complete, and see that storm windows and doors are sound and fit properly.

6. If you have a fireplace, make sure that the flue is clean and that the damper is working properly.

7. After your last watering of shrubs and lawn, shut off your outside faucets to prevent freezing. You do this by *opening* the faucet outside the house, and *shutting* the valve on the same line inside the house.

Winter

1. If you've done all your maintenance jobs as suggested, you should have nothing to contend with except emergencies during the winter. This is a good time to concentrate on inside jobs such as painting, papering, furniture refinishing, and so on.

2. As soon as possible after a storm, check for possible hazards—broken power lines, dangerous ice conditions, and tree limbs that have been weakened and might fall down. Call the proper authorities to handle such emergencies. *Don't go near a fallen power line,* and keep others—particularly children—away from this very dangerous condition.

3. Have candles and flashlight ready for power failures. When power is restored, it sometimes runs at lower than normal voltage for a short while. If a light bulb glows yellow or orange, you can be sure voltage is low. Unplug any motor-powered appliances such as refrigerators, freezers, and washers. A motor will quickly burn out if it is forced to run on voltage substantially lower than what it is designed for.

Play it safe. No discussion of preventive maintenance would be complete without pointing out some of the most important preventive techniques—those of preventing accidents or damage to persons or property. Every time you spot an unsafe condition, *take care of it at once*. A minute or two is a small price to pay if it averts a lifetime of regret.

Fire Safety

This should be uppermost on your mind all the time. Clutter encourages unsafe conditions and makes fires easier to spread. So, the first thing to do is to get rid of accumulated junk.

You should know better than to let oily rags lie around in corners just inviting trouble. Unfortunately, most fires happen to people who should have known better, but were just neglectful in taking care of unsafe conditions in time to prevent a tragedy.

Flammables can't be eliminated completely from an efficient household. They include oil-based paints and solvents, a small amount of gasoline for power garden equipment, and even home barbecue lighter fluids. Make sure all such flammables are covered tightly when not in use and away from sources of heat and flame.

One thing often overlooked is the fact that certain appliances generate heat which should be ventilated away. A refrigerator needs space to dissipate the heat it is removing from inside the cabinet. Appliances or tools run with electric motors should not be overloaded because of the heat generated in such an operating condition.

The list for fire safety could go on and on. However, most of the precautions are plain common sense. If you think you need help in identifying all the unsafe conditions possible in a modern home, get in touch with your local fire department. They have information that they would be just too delighted to give you.

Personal Safety

Again, a long list of personal safety hints could be prepared if one were so minded. The big reason for accidents is seldom the fact that a person is unaware that a hazard exists, but rather a "take a chance" attitude in order to save time. Everyone thinks an accident will happen to someone else. Well—*it can happen to you.*

In your preventive maintenance check inside and outside your house, all the obvious unsafe conditions should get top priority on your list of things to do. It is much more important to fix a broken handrail than to paint the porch.

There are also articles around a house that contribute a lot to accidents—ladders, dangerous chemicals, and certain power tools. One way of minimizing hazards with these objects is to take the time, when you acquire them, to make a safe place to store them. Ladders can be hung out of the way of traffic in your garage; paint removers, bleaches, and acids should go in some sort of secure cabinet with a door; and things like glass storm windows and doors should be stored so people won't run into them and cut themselves with broken glass.

Finally, don't take chances where safety is involved; the risk simply isn't worth it. The seven tools we emphasize throughout this book are about as safe as possible. However, it is more than likely that in time you will acquire other, potentially more dangerous tools. You will probably get a power lawn mower or a power saw or any of a dozen other popular, useful, and desirable timesavers. Read the instruction booklet before you take the tool out of the carton. It may save you a finger or some other part of you that isn't replaceable. We want you to be around for the rest of this book.

Chapter 4

EXTERIOR REPAIRS YOU CAN DO

WHETHER THE AREA you live in is blanketed by snow for many months or bathed by the sun for an entire year, your house is under constant attack from man-made and natural elements. The rays of the sun slowly destroy a coat of paint; humidity rots wood; ice splits cement; and industrial fumes can blacken metal siding and dull the finish.

This relentless attack is going on all the time, and it is most important to carry out a program of regular inspection and repair before the elements take their toll. For the most part, keeping ahead of the problems will often mean much less work than what is later required to repair damage which has been neglected.

In this chapter, we will show you how to stay ahead of nature and eliminate the need for expensive carpenters and masons whose services might be required if you let the little problems grow. You can do these jobs with your seven simple tools with some slight improvisation. However, there has been no compromise in terms of the quality of the repair.

Choosing the Right Premixed Cement

Because most of the repairs you will tackle will not require a lot of cement, it is better to buy the pre-mixed material in a bag, rather than to buy and mix separate ingredients. However, there are considerable differences between the various mixtures and their uses. Premixed materials will cost more than buying separate ingredients, but for the small tasks faced by most homeowners, this cost is more than offset by the convenience factor.

Knowing which mix to use for which task is very important. Many a handy person has mixed the wrong materials and ended up with a crumbling project. So, before you buy any premix, read the next few paragraphs very carefully. And keep these things in mind at all times:

- Before you mix water with any premix, be sure to blend the dry contents thoroughly. This is especially important if you do not intend to use the entire contents of one bag at one time.

- Add only the amount of water specified on the bag by the manufacturer, and follow the mixing specifications to the letter. Water should be added slowly and carefully to the dry materials, and mixing should be thorough.

- If the weather is hot and dry, it will be necessary to keep the cement from drying out too fast. Hot, dry weather causes evaporation of the water from freshly poured cement, leaving a weak and crumbly patch. To cure a patch, cover the fresh cement with burlap or canvas and keep it moist for four or five days. If your patch is on a wall, and you can't cover it, give it a fine spray of water several times a day.

Here are various types of premixes and their uses:

Sand Mix.   As the name implies, this is a mixture of sand and cement. It is useful for patches up to 2 inches thick and can be used for patching cracks in cement walks, floors, and stucco walls. It can be used as a base for flagstones and as a reinforcing coat on walls, walks, and steps.

Concrete Mix.   Sometimes called a gravel mix, this material is especially suited for jobs where extra strength is required. It is generally used for pouring collars around fence posts, for steps and sidewalks, and as a base for masonry barbecues. In addition to sand and portland cement, the mixture contains properly sized gravel.

Mortar Mix.   This is a mixture of sand, cement, and lime, and its plasticity makes it very workable. Mortar is used to join bricks, stone, and cinder and concrete block.

Waterproof Mixes.   These mixes contain special waterproofing compounds in addition to sand and cement. They are used on surfaces which are exposed to a lot of water and can be used to repair below-ground foundation cracks to prevent leakage.

Repairing Walks and Steps

Repairing Cracks in Walks.   A crack in a walk in a cold climate can spell disaster. Each time the crack fills with water and freezes, it will get worse. The repair is easily handled with sand mix. First, undercut the crack as much as possible with a point of a can opener so that the bottom of the crack is wider than the opening on the surface. When it is impossible to get a good undercut, you should use a special cement which expands as it sets. This is available at most hardware stores. Using a stiff broom or brush, clean all the loose cement and debris from the crack. Then

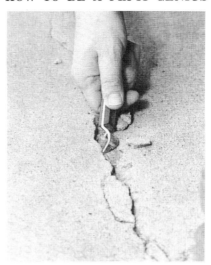

Use a sharp can opener to clean and undercut a crack.

wet down the cracked area so that it is damp, but not running with water. Next, pack freshly prepared cement into the crack with the 4-inch scraper, and level it with a block of wet wood. For the strongest joint, cover the patch with damp burlap for four or five days.

Replacing large pieces of concrete in a sidewalk or patio is handled in the same manner, except that considerably more cement is involved. In this case, a gravel mix is used. However, there is a point beyond which the average handy person should avoid doing masonry work. Simple cracks are easily patched, but replacing large areas should be left to a mason, unless, of course, the idea appeals to you.

Replacing Loose Bricks. When a brick has broken loose from the mortar in a walk or wall, it is repaired by first removing all the old, dry mortar. You can use a hammer and any kind of improvised tool to knock loose the old mortar. Usually the mortar is so loose (that's why the brick became unstuck in the begin-

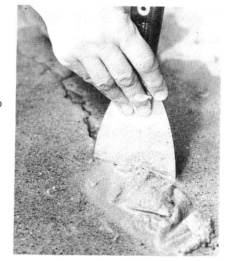

Pack a cement mixture into the crack with the scraper. After 10 minutes or so, level the surface with a wet block of wood.

ning) that even the end of a stick will do the job when tapped sharply with a hammer. Then simply "butter" the ends of the brick with premix mortar and replace.

There are also patching compounds which can be spread on as thin as 1/16 inch and which will do the job if you've loosened all the old mortar that you can. They are sold under many commercial names, but each includes either a latex liquid to be used instead of water or a vinyl binder which is mixed with water. Both work well, and you can use whatever your hardware store dealer recommends. The important point to remember is that no chipping or undercutting has to be done. Be sure to follow the manufacturer's directions carefully. Loose brick or block steps may be repaired with this patching material as well.

Repairing Blacktop Driveways

Holes   Blacktop is essentially a soft material, and it will develop holes in the spots where the excava-

Crumbling mortar on brick joints can often be loosened with a block of wood and a hammer.

After placing a bed of mortar for the brick to rest in, "butter" the side of the brick with mortar to complete the repair.

Use the end of your hammer to tamp the brick into position.

Use the scraper to finish the joints.

tion was soft or where materials such as scrap wood underneath have rotted away. To repair such holes is simply a matter of removing the loose material and filling the hole with commercially available blacktop patching material.

Small holes can be filled directly with the patching material, but larger holes should have some coarse gravel packed tightly in the bottom of the hole before the blacktop is added. This is to save blacktop.

The blacktop patching material is a cold-mix asphalt, and it should be loose to work properly. Generally speaking it won't harden in the bag unless it is left out in the cold. But it is easily loosened by putting the bag in a warm place for a few hours.

Patching should be done in layers. Apply some material, and tamp it firmly into place. Any heavy, flat object can be used as a tamper. Probably the most convenient tamper is the end of a heavy piece of wood such as a two-by-four or a four-by-four. In tamping, make sure that the patching material is pressed firmly into the hole and that it is forced tightly against the sides.

The final filling should bring the patch about ½ inch above the surface of the driveway. This should then be tamped with the wood block and rolled tight by driving over it several times. To prevent sticking, sprinkle a light coating of sand over the patch.

Cracks Cracks in blacktop driveways are easily filled with liquid patching material available at most hardware stores. To fill a small crack, first pour in a little sand, then fill the crack with the liquid sealer.

In filling larger cracks, it is best to mix the patching liquid with sand before pouring it into the crack. A light coat of sand over these patches will protect them and prevent them from sticking to shoes and tires which ride over them.

Sealing the Entire Surface of a Blacktop Driveway If the entire driveway is to be resurfaced, you can use any of the many blacktop sealers available. However, all the holes should have first been patched and the cracks filled.

Begin this job by first brushing the drive down completely. Any grease spots should be lifted off with the 4-inch scraper, and oily areas should be thoroughly scrubbed with a strong detergent. When the surface is patched and clean, wet it down with a garden hose. The entire surface should be wet, but there should be no puddles. After the sealer has been thoroughly stirred, it should be poured on in small quantities and spread evenly on the damp driveway with an old pushbroom. A light coat is usually all that will be needed, and it should dry overnight. However, for a driveway in very poor condition, it may be necessary to apply a second coat. This should not be done until the first coat is thoroughly dry.

SOLVING DRAINAGE PROBLEMS

When it rains, a lot of water can fall on the roof of a house. If the water is allowed simply to run off the roof and fall at the point where the foundation enters the ground, there can be serious leakage problems. To prevent this, gutters are installed at the edge of roofs, and downspout drains are connected to them to carry the water off the roof and away from the house. Some downspouts are connected to storm sewers by means of underground drains. Some are connected to dry wells at some distance from the house, and others use plastic or cement splash pans to carry the water at least a few feet from the house. There are still other devices which can be used to keep water from the foundation, such as a coiled plastic sleeve that connects to the downspout and uncoils as it fills with water, leading the water a safe distance from the foundation.

Whatever system is used, it must be kept in top shape if the basement is to stay dry during periods of rain. And the most neglected portion of the whole water-removal system is usually the gutter and the downspout.

Repairing Rain Gutters

Here's where a little regular maintenance can save you a lot of future work. Gutters which are allowed to remain full of leaves and other debris will quickly clog. Water will spill over the edge and may find its way into the cellar. It can also wet the fascia board so that it will eventually rot and require replacement. And the gutters themselves will deteriorate and have to be replaced.

Gutters should be thoroughly cleaned at least twice a year—once in the fall after all the leaves have fallen, and once again in spring. If you have a lot of trees nearby and overhead, it may be necessary to do this cleaning more often.

To prevent leaves and twigs from entering and evenutally clogging the downspout, it is a good idea to install commercially available wire leaf strainers. These are pushed into the downspout opening in the gutter just enough to be snug. Do not force them in flush with the bottom surface of the gutter. There are also screens which will cover the length of the gutter.

Gutters are made of wood, plastic, steel, copper, and aluminum. Wooden gutters will last a long time with proper care. This is simply a matter of coating the inside of the gutter with linseed oil every year. But you must do the job when the gutter is thoroughly dry. Wait for at least four or five hot, dry days after the last rain to do this job. The outside of the gutter should be painted with ordinary house paint each time the house itself is painted.

Even though metal gutters won't rot, they do oxidize and should receive occasional attention. This is best handled by applying a good coat of varnish to the inside surfaces after they have been thoroughly cleaned. You can also use a liquid roofing coating.

Repairing Sagging Gutters Gutters are installed so that they slope off toward the downspout at a rate of about ⅛ inch per foot. When snow or ice bends the gutter beyond this pitch, it should be repaired to prevent the possibility of serious water damage.

Repairing a strap-hung type of gutter is simply a matter of removing and repositioning the straps to give the gutter the proper pitch. These straps are placed under the first course of shingles. Never nail a strap on top of a shingle. Water will find its way to the nail and into the house. It also looks terrible.

The other types of gutter hangers may have to be removed and repositioned to get the correct slope, but before this job is tackled, you should determine if the gutter is bent or the hangers are out of position. More often than not, heavy ice has simply bent the gutter, and some slight bending will put it back in position without the need to remove it.

Repairing Holes in Gutters When wooden gutters begin to rot, they can be temporarily patched with thick roofing compound, or sections can be cut out and replaced. Eventually, a rotting wood gutter should be replaced. These days, wood gutters are hard to get, and when they are available, they are expensive. They are also more difficult to install than any of the metal varieties. Therefore, we suggest replacement with any of the metal types. The aluminum gutters are most common and, for the most part, easiest to install. Replacement of gutters is covered in the next section.

Holes in metal gutters are easy to repair, but it is first necessary to clean the areas around the hole thoroughly. After cleaning, brighten the metal with some kitchen steel wool. Use the kind that doesn't have soap inside.

When the area has been thoroughly prepared, lay down a coating of asphalt cement for a few inches all around the hole. A piece of heavy aluminum foil, sheet metal, or canvas should then be laid on the asphalt, over the hole. A second coat is applied over the patch and laid at least an inch beyond the edge of the patch.

Replacing Rain Gutters As we mentioned, a number of different types of gutter material are available, but the easiest to work with and most adaptable seems to be aluminum. These systems come with various hangers and connectors and just about every shape of downspout you could want. Aluminum is easy to work with; you can cut it quickly and cleanly with the hacksaw blade of your turret saw, and you can bend the connectors with your pliers. Some aluminum gutters are hung by using a spike and sleeve arrangement; others are installed with either strap hangers or wall-mounted brackets. Whichever system you select, these gutters are easy to install—if you follow the directions available from your dealer.

Aluminum gutters come in standard 10-foot lengths. They are joined by special clips. There must be a downspout at least every 35 feet, and short sections of gutter are sold with an outlet containing a short pipe which extends downward. This fits into the downspout to carry the water to the ground. If your gutter must make a corner, don't worry; standard miters are available, and they clip together the same way as the main sections. When you come to the end of the gutter, it must be sealed, but again, the manufacturers have provided clip-on caps for this purpose. But right and left are different, so be sure to order the right number of each.

If you are replacing an old system, it is best to measure the length of all existing gutters and downspouts and make a drawing of the system. Be sure to include all miters and downspout sections that will be needed. Include the number of caps to seal the ends, the number of slip-joint connectors to join the gutter sections, and the decorative straps that hold each downspout against the side of the house. If this is the first time you have worked with aluminum gutters, add about a foot to the final figure you get for the gutter and downspout material. This will give you some room to practice cutting and working with the material. It won't take long to become expert in working with aluminum, but you don't want to do it on material which will be used, where a mistake could ruin the appearance of the house.

The spike and sleeve system is most easily mastered. Spikes should be spaced every 32 inches, or in every other rafter. First holes must be drilled to take the diameter of the spike in both the front and back of the gutter near the edges. The spike is pushed through the front hole, into the sleeve, and out the hole in the back. Then the spike is driven into the fascia board. Now, this is most important: The gutter must slope toward the downspout at a rate of about 1 inch for every 8 feet. For especially long runs of gutter—40 feet or more—there should be a high point in the middle with the gutter sloping off at both ends to separate downspouts. One final touch: Make sure that the outer edge of the gutter is below the edge of the roof. This is easily done by using a straightedge during construction and laying it on the roof so that it overhangs the edge. Position the gutter just below the straightedge.

All the connectors should be positioned on the ground and sealed with a special aluminum caulking compound which will be available from the store which sells the gutters. If you are working by yourself, you can use large nails driven part way

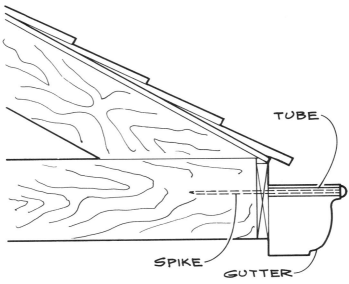

How aluminum gutters are installed.

into the fascia to support an end while you are making connections.

The illustration on this page shows the various parts and how they are assembled. If you plan carefully and follow these instructions, installing new gutters will be a relatively easy job.

SIMPLE ROOF REPAIRS

Tracing a water spot in an upstairs room to a point on the roof where the rain has entered can be a tough job. Very seldom does the water spot occur directly under the hole. More often than not, leaks can be traced to defective flashing on a chimney or around vent pipes. If these points can't be easily sealed with roofing cement, it is best to call in a competent roofing contractor to do the job.

To find the origin of a leak, you will have to wait for

a rainstorm and spend your time in the attic looking for leaks. If the attic is unfinished or uninsulated, you should be able to locate the leak; but if it is covered with insulation batts, wallboard, or any other finishing material, you will either have to remove it or seek a professional to handle the job.

Let's assume that you can see the underside of the roof. It will take a very careful search with a flashlight to find a leak. Once you spot water, you will have to follow it to its source, which is often over rafters and up the inside of the roof. When you have spotted the point of entry, drive a thin nail up through the roof so that it protrudes outside on the surface of the roof. This will enable you to locate the spot which must be repaired after the rain has stopped.

Climbing a roof requires caution. Wear soft-soled shoes like sneakers, and try to avoid stepping on the edge of the shingles. They can be easily cracked, and this can add further to leakage problems. It is best to work on asphalt shingles in warm weather, as it will be necessary to lift some shingles, and a warm shingle will bend and be less likely to crack than a cold, brittle shingle.

Repairing and Replacing Asphalt Shingles

You will need your screwdriver to lift the heads of old shingle nails, a hammer, your putty knife, a handful of special galvanized roofing nails, and replacement shingles.

Begin by carefully lifting the shingle *above* the shingle to be replaced. With your screwdriver, lift the heads of the nails holding the damaged shingle down, and finish the removal with the claw of the hammer. You should then be able to pull out the old shingle. Next, slide the new shingle into place under the lifted shingle. If it binds, you may have to do some minor trimming. Binding usually occurs where nails from the shingles above interfere with the placement. Trim gingerly, in small steps. Once the shingle is in position, nail it down with the flat-head roofing nails, and cover the heads with a little roofing cement.

Lifted, curled, or ripped shingles can often be repaired without the need for replacement. Apply a liberal coat of roofing cement under the shingle, and press it in position.

If replacement shingles are not available, it is often possible to make a good repair by sliding a sheet of copper or aluminum under the damaged shingle. The bottom of the piece of metal should be coated with roofing cement, and it should be forced up completely under the damaged shingle.

Making Repairs to a Flat Roof

A flat roof is one which is not quite as steeply pitched as other roofs, but it is nevertheless slightly pitched to carry off the rain. Flat roofs are seldom covered with individual shingles, but rather with large sheets of roofing material which is supplied to the builder in rolls. The roof is first covered with tar paper and a coat of roofing compound, and then the roofing material is applied in long sheets.

These roofs often blister, but repairs are simple. First cut through the blister with your pocketknife, being careful not to cut the tar paper below. Next, using the 4-inch scraper, push roofing cement under each side of the cut, and then nail down the sides with flat-head roofing nails. Cover this area with roofing cement, and then apply a patch made of either tar paper or shingle over the area. Nail the patch down with roofing nails, cover it and about an inch of the surrounding area with roofing cement, and the patch is done.

If the entire roof needs resurfacing, cover it with asphalt roof paint, which can be applied with an old broom. Roof paint is messy to work with. Take care that it doesn't run off on the sides of the house. Make sure that you have thoroughly brushed the surface of the roof clean before applying the paint. A 5-gallon bucket of this paint should cover about 100 square feet.

EXTERIOR FOUNDATION REPAIRS

Cracks can appear in a foundation for several reasons. Some cracks can be easily fixed by the home handy person, but others do require the attention of a competent contractor.

If you notice large cracks in foundation walls, serious settling has taken place, and a contractor should be called to correct the situation. This often requires more than simply filling the crack. If the foundation is settling unevenly, it may require the pouring of new footings or special shoring of the existing structure. Both jobs are beyond you and your seven simple tools.

But you can and should repair the small cracks which occur above the surface and sometimes run slightly below the surface of the ground. Most block foundations are given a finishing layer of mortar which is called the "plaster" coat. This not only produces a better appearance, but also prevents subsoil water from entering the pores of the foundation blocks. Very often the block and the mortar expand at different rates; when this occurs, something gives and results in cracks in the plaster coat. These cracks are easily fixed.

Rake out the crack with your can opener, and then clean the crack with a stiff brush. Wet it down, and apply a fresh mixture of mortar, using your scraper. It may be necessary to cure this patch by dampening it for a few days, because the water in the mortar will be quickly absorbed by neighboring block and cement.

Wood Rot and How to Prevent It

There are tiny microorganisms, similar to fungus, that can cause serious damage to a house. These organisms can only survive where there is moisture. Favorite spots include the fascia board behind a wood gutter on the north side of a house (where the sun can't dry out the wood), places where wood touches the ground, or any other spot where wood is regularly exposed to dampness.

A preservative can be applied to new work to prevent this from happening. Preservative can also be applied to wood which has been attacked by rot. It won't restore the wood to its original condition, but it will arrest any further attack. Of course, if the wood has seriously deteriorated, it should be replaced.

The chemical is pentachlorophenol, usually referred to simply as penta. If you are doing new work, it is best to soak the wood before construction. Fence posts, door sills, and other wood parts which will be exposed should be so treated. If soaking is impossible, a sprayed or brushed-on coat is the next best thing.

If you are applying a preservative to new woodwork and plan to paint it, ask your hardware dealer to give you a version of preservative which also acts as a paint primer. There are a number of brands of this material available, and all work equally well.

In addition to using these products on parts of your house, you should also consider applying a coat to any outdoor wooden garden furniture you have as well as to wooden ladders and trellises.

A word of caution: Apply these chemicals in a well-ventilated space, and if possible use a filter-type mask. Also, try not to get any of the material on your skin. It is irritating to most people, but its effects can be minimized by immediately washing with warm water and soap.

EXTERIOR WALL REPAIRS

Caulking Cracks

Nothing in a house is continuous; that is, everything must be joined to something else. In fact, old-time carpenters used to be called *joiners*. And where joints are made, there is always the possibility of a water leak, an air leak, an entrance for bugs, and even the loss of expensively produced heat during the winter. There is one simple solution to this problem, and it is caulking.

Caulking compound is a blend of oils, pigments, and a putty base which is ordinarily available in black, white, and gray colors. It can also be supplied in other colors to match some paints. Caulking compound has several characteristics which make it very helpful for the handy person. It will stick to just about every kind of building material, and it will remain elastic for a long time. This elasticity is important because as temperature changes, materials expand and contract. When cracks and joints are properly caulked, they will not open to the outside. And one job provides considerable protection.

You can buy caulking compound in a variety of containers: in cartridges for special guns, in bulk cans, in tubes which often include a neat roll-up key to make it work like a gun, and in rolled-up rope form. We suggest that for smaller caulking jobs, you buy either the rope or tube version. If you have more and larger voids to fill, consider bulk quantities in either quarts or gallons, or rent a gun and use cartridges.

All new houses are caulked to fill open joints, but this application will in time dry and no longer be effective. Before these cracks are resealed it is important that the openings be carefully prepared first. Caulking compound simply will not stick to damp, dirty, or greasy surfaces. Begin by scraping out all the old caulking with a knife or can opener and cleaning vigorously with a stiff brush. An old whisk broom from the linen closet is most handy for this job. A narrow crack should be opened to a V shape with the point of your can opener. Then you should apply the brush again. Joints near chimneys serving an oil burner often have a thin film of sooty oil on them. This surface will not hold the caulking, so it is important that the area be thoroughly wiped down with a solvent such as paint thinner.

Here are some of the more important areas which should be carefully caulked on the outside of the home:

- Where siding meets window and door frames
- Where masonry meets siding, such as at chimneys, steps, and porches
- At all points of roof flashing
- Underneath windowsills
- At corners where siding meets
- Under roof eaves at the gable molding
- And anywhere else where leaks of air and water might occur

Whatever kind of caulking you buy—can, rope, or tube—use your thumb to produce a convex rather than concave surface. It may be necessary to push material into the crack with your scraper, but it is important to leave the outer surface as a convex shape which is less likely to crack when expansion take place than a concave or flat finish.

If you're faced with an especially large crack to fill, don't waste a lot of caulking on the operation. Buy some oakum, which is a ropelike material designed for just such filling operations. After the crack has been packed tightly with the oakum, finish the surface with a layer of caulking compound.

Caulking can also be used to fill small cracks in stucco walls and other siding material. And it can be used to seal holes where pipes leave the house, such as external water connections and conduit for outside wiring.

Repairing Brick and Mortar Joints

Bricks will outlast most other building materials, but the mortar which holds them together is somewhat less enduring. The mortar joints can crack and crumble, often opening the house to serious leakage problems. It is easy for the handy person to repair minor problems with brick and mortar, but serious problems should be referred to a mason.

In describing these repairs, we have had to adapt two tools for jobs for which they were not designed, and those who lay bricks for a living will scoff. We have substituted the 4-inch scraper for a mason's trowel and the can opener for a cold chisel. More of this as the work progresses.

To repair a cracked or crumbling mortar joint between bricks, it is first necessary to remove the old, loose mortar. To do this, first scrape the area with the can opener. If the mortar is crumbly enough, a few hard pulls may do the job. But, more than likely, it will be necessary to use the can opener and hammer in chisel fashion. To do this, place the point of the can opener on the area to be broken up, and hold the can-opener handle parallel to the face of the wall. Then hit the head of the can opener, and drag the opener through the joint. A few passes should be enough to do the job. However, be careful not to damage any of the brick in the process. When all the crumbling mortar has been loosened, sweep it out with a stiff brush.

You are now ready to apply mortar with the next of the improvised tools—the scraper. It is best to use premixed mortar and to prepare it on a piece of dampened plywood. You will know when it is at the right consistency when it will stand by itself and not sag when piled on your scraper.

The area to be repaired should have been thoroughly dampened—wet, but not running with water. Using the edge of the scraper, begin filling the voids between the bricks which you have just prepared. Try to avoid getting any of the mortar on the face of the brick. After a little practice, this will be quite simple.

After you have filled a few rows—usually 5 to 10 minutes—you should then finish off the new mortar to match the style of the original work. To make a concave finish, draw a dampened wooden dowel or your fingertip through the joint, and clear the forced-out mortar away with the scraper. Tapered or beveled joints can be made by drawing the edge of the scraper through the joint to simulate the original construction style. This process is called "striking" by masons; it not only makes a pretty joint, but also contributes to the strength of the joint by compacting it.

When bricks themselves are cracked, and large cracks appear to run through both the brick and the mortar, it is important to call in a professional. This problem often requires more than just patching.

How to Clean Masonry

Brick, stone, and cement all have a somewhat rough surface which traps and holds dirt. This makes it extremely difficult to clean, but the application of a mixture of water and muriatic acid will often do the job. Muriatic acid is available in most hardware and paint stores, and it should be mixed with about 3 parts of water.

Use a stiff brush, such as a laundry brush, but be sure to use rubber gloves for this work. It's also a good idea to wear some form of eye protection such as sunglasses or safety goggles. If you happen to get some on your skin, wash it off quickly with water. And avoid breathing the vapors.

After a vigorous scrubbing, allow the acid solution to rest for about 15 minutes before flushing heavily with fresh water. The garden hose is best for this job because it has force and can penetrate the cracks and pores of the masonry.

Smoke stains on chimneys and fireplaces can be removed by scrubbing with trisodium phosphate, available in hardware and paint stores. This common material is the base for many cleaners sold for considerably more money under commercial brand names.

Mix about ½ pound with a gallon of hot water, and scrub the stained surface briskly with a stiff brush. Rinse the area after the scrubbing with clear, fresh water. These stains are difficult to remove completely, but you should be able to get rid of most of them, or at least turn some very black areas to a less ugly gray.

REPAIRING WOOD AND STUCCO SIDING

Replacing Broken Wood Shingles

Wood shingles can split, warp, and bulge. Before going to the trouble of trying to replace a shingle which has any of these problems, it is best to try to fix the condition by using the original shingle. Begin by resetting nails which may have pulled loose. If rehammered nails fail to hold, try driving a new nail near the old nail. Be sure to use only rustproof nails which are sold expressly for hanging shingles. In most cases, these remedies will serve the purpose.

However, if they don't, it's not that difficult to remove and replace a shingle.

Using the hacksaw blade of your turret saw, cut through the nails that hold the top of the damaged shingle. This is done by sliding the blade up under the shingle above the damaged shingle until the nails are felt. You will also have to cut the nails which hold the bottom of the shingle in the same manner. When all of the nails have been cut, lift the bottom of the damaged shingle and pull it straight down.

You may not be able to pull the entire shingle out as one piece. If this occurs, split the shingle in several places using your hammer and can opener—but be very careful not to damage adjacent shingles which are in good condition.

When the shingle has been completely removed, use either your hammer claw or pliers to remove the old nails. Then slide a new shingle in place, and nail it top and bottom as was the old shingle. Pulling out an old shingle can sometimes damage the tar paper which is often laid on the wall before shingling. If the paper is damaged, cut a new piece of tar paper and lay it in place before adding the new shingle.

Replacing Asbestos Shingles

Seldom do asbestos shingles require repair. They are not subject to the same problems which cause wood shingles to rot, crack, and warp. But they can be damaged when struck, and this is the most common cause of replacement.

Asbestos shingles are removed the same way as wood shingles. Only remember this: Wood shingles have some give and can bend, but asbestos shingles are stiff and brittle. If you are lifting a good shingle above the damaged shingle in order to slip in your hacksaw blade, you may crack a good shingle.

Unlike wood shingles, asbestos shingles are nailed only along the butt end, or bottom edge. The shingle is simply slid under the shingle above and nailed in place. But it is important to remember this: You can drive a nail through a wood shingle, but an asbestos shingle should have a predrilled hole for the nail. Use your twist drill to make the hole. And when the head of the nail gets close to the face of the shingle, be sure that you are making flat strokes so that the head of the hammer is parallel with the shingle. A whack with the *edge* of the hammerhead can give you what you already have—a cracked shingle. If you bought the bell-faced type of hammer we suggested in Chapter 1, and are using a full-arm swing, you should have no problems with this job.

Repairing and Replacing Clapboard

Clapboard, like any other wood, can split. And when it does, it will let dampness in behind it that can cause rot at worst and no less than a case of peeling paint on the surface. It the cracks are small and don't appear to endanger a complete length of board, they can be filled with caulking compound. This operation should be completed by hammering in the existing nails, or adding nails if needed to keep the crack from spreading. If the wood is dry and might split when nailed, it's always best to drill a small pilot hole for the nail in the clapboard.

Larger cracks can be repaired, but the job requires more than an application of caulking compound. Begin by prying the loose portion of board out so that the surface edge of the crack is exposed. This can be done with either the scraper or the screwdriver. Then apply a coat of good waterproof glue to the edges. The glued joint should be held tightly while it dries, and the best way to do this is to lightly nail a block of wood tightly up against the lower edge of the glued clapboard. Do not drive the nails all the way in when doing this. Hold the block firmly against the lower edge, and drive the nails in only far enough to hold.

Then give the block a few taps to tighten it against the clapboard, and let the glue set as recommended by the manufacturer. When the glue dries, remove the block and fill the nail holes with putty.

When a run of clapboard is badly cracked, it must be removed and replaced. Begin by marking off the area to be replaced and drawing pencil lines perpendicular from the bottom of the course of clapboard above to outline the area to be removed—and to act as saw guides.

The damaged section of clapboard should be lifted away from the course of board below by wedging small scraps of wood under the butt end. Then, using the wood-cutting blade of your turret saw, cut along the lines you have drawn until you are through the wood. You must be careful in doing this not to cut into the board below. The nails in the butt end will have to be cut out with the hacksaw blade, as we described in the section on removal of shingles. Now, remove the wedges and push them under the board above the damaged clapboard. You should now be able to break off, by hand, a major portion of the damaged board.

When this has been done, it will be necessary to use the hacksaw under the upper board to cut free the remaining nails. The last pieces of damaged clapboard should then be easy to remove by simply prying with your screwdriver.

Once the damaged section of clapboard has been removed, you should make a thorough inspection of the surface below. If the crack has been open for a long while, there may be rot on the wood below. In that case, you should really have a carpenter inspect the job. It might require professional attention, well beyond you and your seven simple tools.

If there is no rot, check the condition of the tar paper before replacing the clapboard. Small rips and cuts can be repaired by applying roofing cement, but large damaged sections should be replaced with new tar paper. Tar paper is nailed down with flat-head roofing nails, and the new edges should be sealed with roofing cement.

You are now ready to replace the section of clapboard, and if you made the cuts parallel as we described, the new piece should slide right in place, leaving no large gaps with the neighboring board. The new section should be tapped in place using a small block of wood and a hammer. Place the block of wood against the lower edge of the clapboard, and tap with the hammer. This will prevent marring the edge of the new piece of board.

Once in place, the new board should be nailed about 1 inch from the bottom edge. Then the top edge is fastened by nailing through the lower edge of the course of board above. If the old course is dry, it is best to drive pilot holes for the nails first. The nails should be countersunk—that is, driven so that the heads are slightly below the surface of the board. Ordinarily, this is done with a tool called a nail set, but your bag of tools doesn't include this instrument. No matter; it can be done by using a larger nail. Simply place the tip of the larger nail in the center of the head of the nail to be countersunk, and drive it in a little farther.

Next, coat the new board with a layer of exterior priming paint. When this has dried, the joints should be filled with caulking compound, and the countersunk nails covered with putty. A final coat of exterior paint can then be applied to blend with the paint on the surrounding surface.

Repairing Cracks in Stucco

Smaller cracks in stucco are easily repaired with the tools you have, but large damaged areas do require the attention of a mason.

Use premixed mortar for stucco crack repairs, and if you don't plan to use all the material in one bag, thoroughly mix the dry cement in the bag before you add water. If the wall you are working on is colored stucco, you will have to get pigment to add to the mortar mix. These pigments are usually available in hardware and paint stores. When mixing the pigment with the mortar, you must be sure that the pigment weight never exceeds 5 percent of the mortar mix. The chances are that you will never reach this level under ordinary circumstances, but when trying to match a dark wall there can be a tendency to add more pigment than is really required.

Begin the repair by widening the crack with your can opener and hammer. It will be necessary to get an undercut to make a good joint. This is done by pushing the point of the can opener under the edge of the crack, then dragging it through the crack slowly while tapping it with a hammer. Once the crack has been prepared, use a stiff brush to remove all loose particles, and then dampen the crack and surrounding area.

The premixed mortar should be mixed so that it is workable, yet firm enough to be piled. If it settles, add just enough dry mortar to make it the right consistency. Follow the mixing instructions on the bag.

Work the mortar into the crack with your scraper, packing it tightly. Then use the scraper to smooth the patch even with the surrounding stucco. If the crack is fairly large, it is a good idea to lightly dampen it daily for two or three days. A fine mist from the garden hose will do the job.

WINDOW REPAIRS

Unsticking double-hung Windows

A double-hung window is made of wood and has two sashes—one on the top which pulls down and one below which pushes up. Some of these windows are

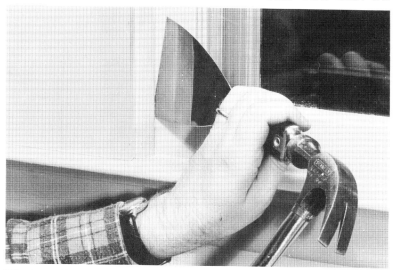

Windows that are painted shut can be loosened with the scraper and light taps from the hammer.

balanced with counterweights inside the casement, and others are balanced by spring lifts. Spring-lift windows can be identified by the metal tube which runs down the casing channel. Sash-weight windows can be spotted by the rope or chain in the channel which disappears over a pulley at the top of the casement. Both types of windows are subject to the same kind of sticking, and both are curable with the same measures.

The most common cause of sticking is paint which has hardened over the window and the frame. If it is only one layer of paint, the quickest remedy is to use a single-edge razor blade to slice open the joint. Be careful not to cut into the wood. Once the window has been freed, it is a good idea to slide the sash either up or down (depending on which sash was stuck) and to smooth the sliced paint edge with a light rubbing of fine sandpaper. Don't take the paint down to the wood; just smooth the edges.

If the window has been painted many times and the razor-blade trick doesn't work, you will have to use your 4-inch putty knife. Place the blade at the edge— as close as possible to the parallel plain of the sash— and lightly tap the handle with your hammer until the blade cuts through the paint. You will have to continue this until all the paint has been opened and the window is free. You should, of course, sand the edges of the cut paint as we described above.

You may find that even after you have cut through the paint, it will be impossible to open the window. There is one thing *not* to do. Do not use the scraper as a wedge to lift the window. The chances are better than even that you will permanently bend the blade. Rather, use the wide blade of your screwdriver over a small stick or dowel for leverage, and pry gently all across the bottom of the sash. If you pry too hard at one spot, you will only succeed in nicking the edge of the sash.

Double-hung windows can stick as the result of excessive humidity which causes the wood to swell and bind. If this is a temporary condition, resulting from a spell of damp weather, the best remedy is to simply wax the edges of the stops and the channel of the window frame. There are aerosol and stick products for just this use, but you can effect a good temporary solution by rubbing a candle, a paraffin block, or even a little soap on the swollen wood.

If the lubrication approach has little effect, you can try tapping the stop molding (the wood strip which presses against the sash when it is closed) with a hammer and a block of wood. A small child's block and your hammer tapped and moved along the complete length of the molding will often solve the problem. Don't use the face of the hammer on the molding directly. You'll nick it and compound the problem.

If both of these measures fail (they seldom do), it will then be necessary to remove the molding and sash and do a light planing. This is beyond the scope of your tool kit and can be a sticky job if you've never done it before. Better leave this to a carpenter.

Casement Window Maintenance

A casement window is made of metal and is hinged to a metal frame. It is often operated by a cranking mechanism which requires occasional attention. You will know the time has arrived when it becomes difficult to open or close the window.

An inspection of the cranking mechanism will be required. Remove the screws which hold the mechanism to the frame. The cranking assembly and the arm will slide out for inspection. Check the gears inside for wear, dirt, and dried lubrication. If the gears are badly worn, the entire assembly will have to be replaced. Take the original unit to a hardware store, and get an exact replacement.

If the mechanism is clogged with dirt and rust, clean it thoroughly by soaking the entire assembly in a solvent such as kerosene. After the gear assembly has been cleaned, it should be repacked with a white, nonstaining grease and replaced on the frame.

If the cranking mechanism is working well, but it is difficult to close a casement window all the way, the problem will often be a collection of dirt and rust in the frame where the window is seated. Use a little kitchen steel wool to clean up the casement and window frame. If you haven't scraped down to the paint, apply a light coat of white grease or other lubricant under the sash.

The hinges are seldom a cause for improper closing by themselves, but they can contribute to the problem. To prevent this from happening, put a few drops of oil in each hinge twice a year. A drop of oil in the crankshaft at the same time will also help forestall problems.

Casement windows are prone to develop air leaks

as they age. This can often be solved by using your monkey wrench to bend the lip of the window frame slightly outward. Do this in very gentle stages to avoid completely distorting the frame.

If you are reluctant to tackle this bending task, you can get commercial weather strips. Some are even made with a self-stick backing to greatly simplify installation.

How to Replace Glass

Broken glass is easily replaced, but the job does take a little care and patience. Begin by removing all the remaining glass, using heavy gloves to avoid being cut.

When all the glass has been removed, the original putty will have to be removed. This is best handled with the scraper, but be careful not to damage the wood surface in the process. While you are removing the old putty, you will come across curious little metal triangles driven into the muntins, or the sash if you are replacing a single-sash pane of glass. These are *glazier's points*, and they are what hold the glass in place—not the putty. They must be removed. You might be able to do this job gingerly so that the same points can be used again, but because glazier's points are so inexpensive, it is just as easy to buy new.

Once the putty and glazier's points have been removed, it will be necessary to sand the opening carefully and to apply either a coat of boiled linseed oil or a light coat of exterior paint. This step is very important; it will prevent the otherwise bare wood from extracting the oil from the new putty when it is applied.

The replacement glass you buy should be about ⅛ inch shorter in both dimensions than the opening in the sash. This not only will make installation easier, but will reduce the possibility of cracking if the frame should become warped.

Use a heavy glove to remove the broken glass.

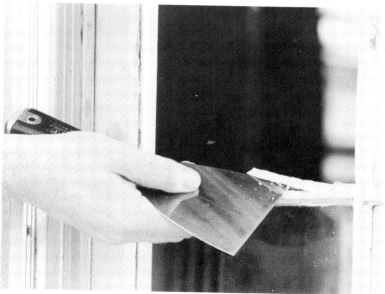

The scraper will easily loosen the old putty.

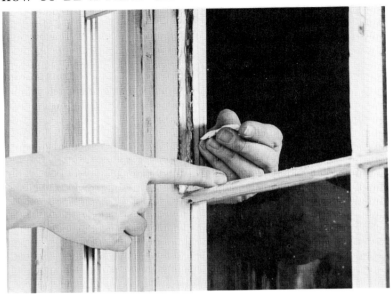

Lay a thin bead of putty in the channel where the glass will go.

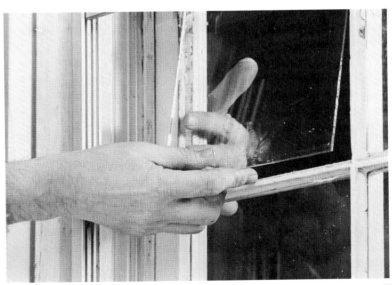

If the new pane is cut about ⅛ inch shorter in each direction, it will slip into place very easily.

Little metal triangles called *glazier's points* are used to hold the glass in place. A setting tool comes with the box of points. Use your hammer with a sliding motion against the glass.

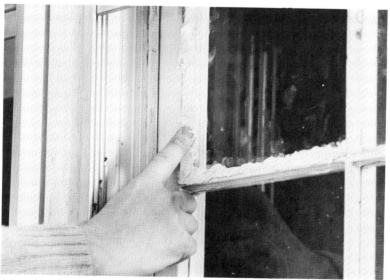

Work a heavy bead of putty all around the glass pane.

After the paint or oil has dried, begin the replacement by applying a light bed of putty or glazing compound along all four sides of the frame. This bedding cushions the glass and prevents leaks. Next, place the new glass against the putty and press firmly along the edges until it is completely in contact with all of the putty and evenly placed.

The glazier's points will have to be installed now. Use the same number of points as you removed, and in approximately the same position. You should use your hammer and screwdriver to place the points, but do this carefully or you will crack the new pane. It won't take much effort to set the points; they are quite sharp and easily driven into the wood. Sometimes a packet of points will include a tool for their installation, but if they don't, the screwdriver and hammer will work just as well.

With the points in and firmly holding the glass in place, the next job is to apply the putty. This is best done by first rolling the putty in strips about the length of each side of the window. The rolled strips should be about ⅜ inch in diameter, or approximately the thickness of an ordinary pencil. Lay one strip in place, and begin to flatten in the same triangular plane as the putty in the other windows with the aid of the scraper. This may take a little getting-used-to, but you should pick it up quickly if you use the scraper firmly and press the putty tightly in place. Excess putty can be cut off with the edge of the scraper or rolled off with the fingers. Once all four sides have been puttied, draw the scraper over the surface of the putty lightly to give it a finished appearance. Try to make the corners sharp and clean. Just copy the look of the putty job in the other panes, and you'll have no problems.

After the new putty has set for at least a week, give it a liberal coat of exterior house paint. Paint up over the putty onto the glass for about 1/16 inch. This acts

Use your scraper to make a neat bevel.

as an extra seal and will help keep the putty from drying.

Replacing Glass in Casement Windows The process of replacing glass in a casement window is essentially the same as that for double-hung wood windows— with one exception. Instead of glazier's points, springs are used to hold the glass in place. Simply use replacement springs and follow the instructions we gave in the last section, and you will be able to replace glass in any casement window.

Repairing Screens

Today, screens are made of a variety of materials, all of them strong, durable, and nonrusting. Metal screens are most often made of aluminum, and sometimes of copper or bronze wire. There are even plastic screens, which are every bit as durable as metal.

Repairing a small hole in either plastic or metal screens can be handled by a dab of any variety of waterproof glue. Before applying the glue, straighten out any bent wire and try to flatten the metal and close the hole as tightly as possible. Use a glue which dries clear, and no one will ever notice the patch.

Larger holes in metal screens can be repaired by making a patch of screening from the same metal. Make the patch about ½ inch larger than the hole on all sides. Then remove wire strands on all sides until the remaining crosshatched screen material is just the size of the hole. Bend the free wires at a right angle, and push them through the openings in the screen surrounding the hole. Squeeze the patch flat, and then bend the wire inward on the other side of the screen. Use waterproof cement to hold the bent wire in place.

Screen and Storm-Window Maintenance

Wood storm windows and screens should be kept well painted. But if excess paint is laid on the sides, the windows will no longer fit in the frames. If this happens, the paint can be removed with coarse sandpaper and the area finished with a light rubbing of fine paper. But to prevent the problem in the first place, it is a good idea when painting to use a specially thinned mixture of paint on the edges of the storms and screens.

Any dried putty on storm windows should be dug out and replaced. It is the dead air space between the storm window and the house sash pane which protects the house, and any leak in the putty will make the storm window inefficient. If storms and screens fit loosely, it is a good idea to buy any of the commercial weather stripping and apply it to the open areas.

If the joints of the wood frames pull loose, you can either glue them together with a good wood glue or use any number of metal mending plates available at your local hardware store. These are screwed in place.

Aluminum storm windows and screens seldom require maintenance, but the tracks should be lubricated occasionally. Aluminum does not rust, but it will pit and oxidize. To keep the surface bright and clean, use any of the commercial preparations available specifically for the job.

Storm doors can be maintained as described for the windows with the addition of the door closer. This device slows the door down as the spring pulls it closed, letting it close firmly but without a bang. The piston-type closer has a small adjusting screw in the end cap. A turn to the left lets the door close faster. A right turn retards the closing speed. Hydraulic door closers are usually mounted at the top of the door frame and are connected by an arm to a plate in the door. The adjusting screw is usually located at the bottom of the cylinder. Push up with the screwdriver, and turn as described above to make any adjustments.

Chapter 5

EASY BASEMENT REPAIRS

BASEMENT REPAIRS ARE usually neglected because they are seldom as pressing or as obvious as problems found in the more lived-in parts of the house. The basement is often thought of as that musty, damp, dark place, filled with spiders, that is only fit for storing household junk.

With very little attention, the average basement can be turned into a pleasant and useful spot. Even if you don't go to the extent of actually building a room, the basement represents a lot of space which is usually badly wasted by most householders. Consider this: With a fully excavated basement, there is as much floor space below the ground as there is on the floor above. And with the exception of the space taken up by the heating plant, it is often possible to do a lot of interesting and very practical things with this part of the house.

Other than spiders and wet laundry, the thing that most often keeps people from using the basement is water. Whether it gushes, trickles, or appears as condensation, water is a very common problem. Except in extreme cases, however, this problem can be cured with very little effort and usually for very little money. But first you should know some things.

HOW WATER GETS INTO BASEMENTS

Basically, there are three ways that water can enter a basement: leakage, seepage, and condensation.

Leakage

Leakage is water trickling through openings; it is most noticeable when there is an actual crack somewhere in the basement wall or floor. Leakage is caused by water from outside the house. If the land is improperly graded (not slanted away from the outside foundation), rainwater will collect, seep into the ground, and find its way into cracks. When the roof gutters or leaders are clogged, water will spill over and fall at the edge of the house. If the land slopes toward the foundation, this water will simply settle into the ground along the foundation and find its way into your basement.

In Chapter 4 we discussed common problems of gutters and leaders. Checking these is always the first step in trying to correct a basement leak. If the gutters and leaders are working and all the rainwater is being carried away from the foundation, there just might be a problem with the subsoil water level. Underground streams and springs have a way of showing up and causing serious problems. If this is the case, there is little you and your simple tools can do. Give in, and call a professional.

Seepage

Water gushing from cracks in cellar walls as leakage is a rare occurrence. Usually the problem of outside water finding its way inside through slow seepage is much more common and is more easily cured. If the cellar walls are intact and there is seepage, it is usually caused by pressure from free water outside or by capillary action drawing water from the surrounding moist soil through porous spots in the wall. Seldom does this problem cause an actual flow or even a trickle of water. More often it results in spotty dampness which appears mostly at the floor wall joint. Seepage is more noticeable after a heavy rain or after snow melts in the spring. If you have the symptoms of seepage at a time when there hasn't been a heavy rain, the problem is one of subsoil flow or a high water table, and it requires professional attention.

Condensation

Put a glass of ice water out on a hot, humid day, and in a very few minutes the outside of the glass will be covered with droplets of water. That's condensation—water which has been wrung from the atmosphere by contact with the cool surface of the glass. The same thing happens in a basement, and this is, by far, the most common cause of that damp, musty smell you get from the head of the cellar stairs.

Condensation can be quite a problem. Sometimes it will look as though it is the result of seepage from the outside. It can show up as damp spots on a cellar wall, and in serious cases, there may be accumulations of water. One way to get a quick feel for this problem is to look for the pipe which brings water into your house. Find the pipe connected to the water meter, and examine it at the point between the meter and the wall after you have run the water for a minute. Bringing cold water through the pipe will lower the temperature, and if there is high humidity in the cellar air, water droplets will form on the outside of the pipe. This is condensation, and similar things are happening on cool basement walls.

If you have damp spots on the wall, or at floor-wall joints where leakage and seepage are most likely to occur, there is one conclusive test to make to see if it is condensation or outside water. Using a dab of putty, chewing gum, or modeling clay, attach a small pocket mirror to the wall where the moisture spot appears. Allow this mirror to stay on the wall for about 12 hours, and then examine it carefully. If the damp spot is still on the wall, and the mirror is clear, then you do have a seepage problem. But if there is a watery fog, or even droplets of water on the mirror, it's condensation.

CURING BASEMENT WATER PROBLEMS

It's always tempting to dig right in and coat the damp spot with something or to plug in a dehumidifier. But before you do anything, make absolutely sure that you know how the water is getting into your basement. And make sure that you have solved all your exterior drainage problems, as outlined in the last chapter. Obviously, if you have water in your basement constantly, or if light rainstorms result in flooding, the problem is beyond you and the seven simple tools. Call in a pro.

Solving Leakage Problems

In one sense, the problem of leakage is simplified in that you can almost always see the source of water. A crack in the wall or an open joint where the wall meets the floor is most often the source.

Once you've located the crack, you will have to do a little work with your beer-can opener. Using the point, pull it through the crack with sufficient force to produce an even groove about ¼ inch wide. Then use the point to undercut each side of the crack. The back of the crack should be wider than the front. If the

The can opener is used to clean out cracks in basement walls.

crack is deep, it may be necessary to go even deeper with the can opener. The object of this is to make the crack wide enough to take the patching material, and the undercut will help hold the patch in place.

When the crack has been prepared, brush it out very carefully to make sure that all the debris is removed. There are many materials you can use to fill the crack. Quite often, ordinary premixed cement will work adequately as a patching compound. The best material is a special cement available in hardware stores for this purpose and sold under a variety of brand names. Most of these products expand, rather than shrink, on hardening and therefore make tight joints.

Mix the cement on a wet board—called a "hawk" by masons. Wetting the board will prevent the extraction of water from the mixture. Also, be sure to wet down the entire area of the crack to be patched. The crack and the adjacent wall should be soaked, but not running with loose water.

The tool you will use here is the scraper. A professional with a big bag of tools would use a regular cement trowel, but you can do the job very nicely with your scraper. Use the scraper to mix the cement on the hawk. The mixture is right when it will hold its own shape when piled up. Force the cement into the crack with the scraper, and push it back to make sure that the crack is completely filled. Also make sure that the undercuts are filled. When you have finished with the filling, use the edge of the scraper to smooth out the patch.

Epoxy fillers form a better bond, and of course a better seal, but they are more expensive. If you have only a small crack to fill, you might consider an epoxy. Because each manufacturer uses a different formulation, follow the instructions printed on the cans for best results.

There are times when a thin crack in the wall will extend right through from the inside to the outside of the foundation wall. If the crack is small enough, and

Use your scraper to force the waterproofing into cracks and holes.

the water pressure is small and sporadic, it is often possible to effect a good cure with one of the commercial liquid latex patches.

Once the crack is located, a trench of 6 to 8 inches is made against the foundation. The ground should then be soaked with water for another 6 to 8 inches. Next, pour in the patcher. Because the latex sets quickly, it is a good idea to spray a light mist of water on the latex surface to prevent a skin from forming. This latex will seep into the crack, set, and provide a good seal. When you see the latex entering the cellar from the inside, you know you've done a good job.

Solving Seepage Problems

Again, before tackling any of the inside remedies, it is wise to make sure that all the outside problems have been eliminated: gutters, leaders, grading, and drainage lines.

When seepage is fairly heavy and the wall is rough concrete block, one of the best solutions is the application of a ¼-inch coat of waterproof cement. This job can be done with your 4-inch scraper, but it will not be easy. A waterproofing chemical is added to the water used to wet a dry blend of 1 part cement and 2½ parts of sand. The wall should be dampened first. Complete the job by applying a coat of portland cement paint.

An easier approach is to use one of the packaged products for this job. Usually the kit includes a quick-setting hydraulic patching compound, a thick base coating, and cement paint. Because of the variations from one manufacturer to another, be sure to follow individual instructions carefully. With most of these materials, the best way to do the job is with an old-fashioned scrub brush borrowed from the laundry. The stiff bristles and a vigorous wrist combine to work in the material for a solid covering.

Where seepage is minimal, an easy out is a coat of

portland cement paint which can be scrubbed on. This can be used over any surface except a surface which has another type of paint. Again, be sure to dampen the walls before applying a coat.

Another solution for minor seepage problems is the application of one of the latex paints made for such a job. Latex paint may be applied over a wall previously covered with cement paint or an earlier coat of latex. In either case, be sure that the walls are clean and free of debris. New concrete should be washed down with a 5 percent solution of trisodium phosphate, which is readily available at most hardware stores.

Solving Condensation Problems

Air that enters a basement brings water with it in the form of vapor. On those hot summer days, the outside air can be loaded with water vapor. When this saturated air reaches the cooler cellar walls, it can no longer hold the water and it condenses on cold surfaces. The most obvious place for condensation to take place is on cold-water pipes and cool walls below the ground level. If the cellar were the same temperature as the air outside, the water vapor would not be able to condense and cause dampness. And that is one of the ways of solving the problem. By keeping cellar doors and windows open during periods of high humidity, the inside and outside temperature will be the same, and there will be little or no condensation. This works, but it does require active monitoring of both the inside and outside temperature to be most effective.

Another way of solving the problem is to seal the cellar as tightly as possible to prevent the entrance of warm, moist air from the outside. This can be done by adding storm windows to the cellar windows and a felt strip to the bottom of the door leading to the first floor. However, even when these measures are taken, moist air will still find its way into the basement. As an additional step to sealing out moist air, it is a good idea to locate the cold-water pipes and either wrap them in fiberglass insulation or cover them with one of the commercially available plastic sleeves which are made for just this purpose. Anything else in the cellar which "sweats" should be covered with at least ¼ inch of mastic. Use the 4-inch scraper for this job.

If you can't reach the pipes, or don't want to bother with the work of covering them, a dehumidifier can be placed in the basement. To be most effective, the dehumidifier should be set up with some type of timer to do its job on a regular basis. And if the unit is not vented to the outside, the water must be removed at least daily.

If a clothes dryer is in use in the basement, make sure that it is vented to the outside. Check it regularly to see that it is not dumping a lot of moist air in the cellar through small leaks in the vent line.

Paneling a basement is a nice touch, but if you have condensation problems you should add a vapor barrier when the paneling is installed. This formidable term is the name for nothing more than a sheet of polyethylene film applied to the back of the paneling. It will keep warm, humid air from reaching the cold foundation wall, where it can condense.

**A Final Word about Basement
Wall Cracks**

It's possible to fix most of the ordinary cracks in basement walls with the scraper and the can opener, but when cracks are noticed around flue pipes (vent pipes leading from the furnace to the chimney), they should be checked by a pro—someone who can determine the possible safety problems and who will use a special mortar for such high-temperature sealing work.

Cracks around incoming water pipes, cellar windows, and sewer lines can be fixed as we described in the section on patching cracks.

TERMITES

Treating a full-scale termite attack is beyond the seven tools—and usually beyond even the most well-equipped handy person. But a twice-yearly inspection of the house can save hundreds or even thousands of dollars in repairs.

Termites live below the ground and abhor anything but the damp, dark environment of their subterranean homes. But they must eat, and their food is the wood in your house, fence, or fireplace log pile. To get to this wood without exposure, they build mud tunnels. The tunnels are especially noticeable along the inside of cellar walls and in crawl spaces, and have even been seen as unsupported columns to reach a piece of wood not in contact with the ground.

But it is possible to have a termite infestation without ever seeing these tubes. Don't think you're safe if you don't see them. Termites can build their tunnels through walls and slab cracks and get directly into the wood to do their dirty work.

If you suspect termites but don't see the tunnels, probe the wood with an ice pick or sharp knitting needle. Uneaten wood will resist the point, but where termites have been active, it will sink in easily. You'll be amazed at how quickly infested wood gives way to the point.

If you do find termites, the best advice we can give you is to seek the help of a termite expert quickly. It's not only a matter of ridding the house of them; it's even more important to find the extent of the damage that has been done.

So, rather than dwell on the various ways of solving

the problem, we think the best advice we can give is that of careful inspection. The following steps, if taken twice a year, will make sure that you catch them early if they do get in. And once they are detected, a professional can clear up the problem for you relatively inexpensively.

1. Termites mate in the spring and early summer. Be on the lookout for large swarms of flying insects. The termite at this stage has two sets of wings, both the same length. The harmless flying ant has two sets of wings, too, but the hind wings are shorter than the forewings. And the body of the termite is approximately the same width from head to tail. The flying ant has a decidedly narrow waist.

2. A pile of discarded termite wings during this same period indicates the establishment of a new colony. Look for the wings around basement walls, in crawl spaces, and near piles of wood.

3. Look for the mud tubes. Favorite spots of the termites include basement walls, cracks in foundations and basement floors, crawl spaces, and wherever wood touches the ground. Be especially watchful of areas where cement slabs touch wood. The tubes are half-round and usually are between ¼ and ½ inch wide.

4. Check doorsills and cellar windowsills. Probe with an ice pick. It is often easy for termites to get to these places without being seen.

5. Wood piled on the ground and untreated fence posts are primary targets for termites. If you find them there, there is a good chance that they are in, or soon will be in, your house. Call the professionals quickly.

Of course, termite exterminators will often provide free inspection service. But with a routine inspection

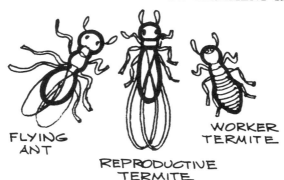

FLYING ANT

REPRODUCTIVE TERMITE

WORKER TERMITE

How to identify termites.

such as we have outlined, the chances are good that you will catch them before any serious damage is done.

Preventing Termites

It is possible to treat the soil around the house to prevent the termites from entering. The termite leaves his underground home only for the cellulose he gets from chewing wood. Once he has chewed it, he must return with it for his comrades, and to get water. Because it is all but impossible to get to his home and destroy him, the best remedy is to make your home unappetizing.

To do this, dig a 2-foot trench completely around the foundation. It doesn't have to be more than 6 or 8 inches wide. Then pour a diluted solution of chlordane into the trench around the entire perimeter of the house. Chlordane is available from any hardware store, and instructions for mixing are on the bottle and should be followed carefully. As the trench is refilled with earth, a small amount of the mixture should be poured on the soil.

When you treat your home, the termite will seek another feast. It is only fair to warn your neighbors of what you have done and to suggest that they do the same or their house will be next on the termite's menu.

LEVELING A SAGGING FLOOR

A sagging floor can cause a variety of problems: wall cracks, sticking windows, and even roof leaks, to mention only a few. The sag may be in the floors above, but the solution to the problem lies in the basement below. Floors can sag for a number of reasons. Faulty original construction, too few supports, a heavy weight in one spot, settling foundation, and shrinking or warping of the beams are only a few of the possible causes. Whatever the cause, the condition should be corrected.

Lifting a sagging floor is best handled by installing a steel jack post. This device is made up of two steel tubes which telescope. The smaller tube, which slides inside the larger, has holes every few inches that hold a heavy steel pin. This hole and pin arrangement is used to adjust the post for the approximate distance between the ceiling and the basement floor. A heavy steel plate is attached to each end, and one end includes a heavy-duty adjusting-screw-type jack for the task of lifting. The basement floor should be at least 4 inches thick to be able to support the work. If it isn't, or if the cement is badly cracked, a mason should be called to remedy the situation.

To use the jack, first place it on the cellar floor below the beam to be lifted. Set the pin and hole to position the top plate as close as possible to the beam above. Then turn the jackscrew gently until there is enough contact to hold the post in position but not to do any lifting. Now it is important to make sure that the jack-post is perfectly vertical and directly under the sagging beam. To do this, tack a weighted string to the beam and let it hang next to the jack-post.

After the string has come to rest, it will be perfectly vertical. Measure the distance between the string and the side of the jack at points near the top and the bottom, and shift the post to make it perfectly vertical. When you are sure that it is absolutely vertical, either nail or screw the plate to the beam above to prevent slipping.

Once the jack is in position and secured, you can begin adjusting the jackscrew. It is very important that this operation be done in gradual stages or you may do serious damage to the house. Turn the screw until there is only slight pressure and then wait for at least 24 hours. Then the adjustments should be limited to only one-half turn a week until the sag has been corrected. It may take weeks or months to get the floor back to its level position, but this is the only way to prevent damaging the house.

If there are any water or gas pipes attached to the beam being lifted, watch them carefully. The lifting process may crack them.

Now, let's look at the problems you can have with floors and stairs and see how to solve them with your seven simple tools.

Chapter 6

FLOORS AND STAIRS

FLOORS AND STAIRS probably get more wear and abuse than any other part of your house. It makes sense, then, to know how to take care of them so they will give you long-lasting, good-looking service.

The best care you can give any floor is to keep it clean. Dirt and grit tracked in from the outside are very abrasive and quickly wear down even the best finish. Frequent dusting or vacuuming, together with regular waxing, will keep most floors good looking for years. But if your floors do need repairs, here are some of the things you can handle yourself.

WOOD FLOORS

Hardwood floors are more susceptible to damage than some of the newer types of flooring materials. In addition to normal wear and accidental damage, wood floors are liable to damage from moisture and water. Make sure you clean wood floors with a product designed for such application. If you must use water to clean up spills (such as milk), use it sparingly and wipe up excess water at once. A puddle of water on a wood floor will ruin the finish, swell the wood fibers, and possibly even cause squeaks.

Turpentine is a very good cleaner for stubborn marks and stains on wood floors. A turpentine-based paste or liquid wax will also do a good job, particularly if you use some fine steel wool. Mildly worn spots can be taken care of very nicely with such a wax treatment.

Patching Worn Spots

With turpentine and clean rags, clean off all old wax in the immediate area of the place you want to patch. Then sand lightly with fine sandpaper on a flat block of wood, making sure you sand with the grain and overlap into the unworn portion of the floor. Then finish the bare area with shellac or other type of wood floor finish. Some of these finishes are available in spray cans which make blending in the edges quite easy. Use several light coats and then wax when dry.

If the wood is very badly worn and stained, you will have to bleach the wood to make it presentable. Hardware stores sell such bleach, but you should be warned that it can be dangerous. It might make better sense to call in a flooring expert who can sand worn spots with a sanding machine. You can even rent such a machine yourself if you have the ambition to try refinishing a whole floor.

Eliminating Squeaks

A big cause of squeaks in an older home is a sagging floor. If this is the case, you should consider jacking up the joists as was suggested in Chapter 5. To eliminate squeaks in other ways, just remember that every squeak is caused by two or more pieces of wood rubbing against one another. The key is to stop all motion that will result in rubbing and squeaking.

Recall how your floors are constructed: long beams called joists span the length of the room and are

Lightly worn spots can be cleaned up with a block of wood and sand-paper. Heavily trafficked areas can be handled with a rented power sander.

After sanding, the area should be cleaned with alcohol.

Spray several light coats of shellac over the sanded area to renew the appearance.

supported on the foundation walls and main girders. On top of these joists is laid the subfloor. The subfloor consists of diagonally laid planks nailed to every joist or sheets of rough plywood nailed the same way. On top of the subfloor, the finish floor is installed. It may be a hardwood floor nailed into the subfloor and the joists underneath, or it may be a composition floor glued to the subflooring with cement.

Squeaks may be caused by:

1. Subflooring which has lifted off the joists
2. Finish wood floors which have lifted off the subfloor
3. Rubbing of the X-shaped bridging members nailed between the joists

The solutions are really quite simple. If the subflooring has lifted off the joists, don't try to nail it

Squeaks can often be eliminated if you drive wedges between the top
of the joist and the subflooring. This can only be done if you can get
at the floor from underneath.

down. Usually the joist has warped and nailing won't
do much good. Rather, cut some thin wedges from a
scrap of wood and hammer them tightly in the spaces
between the subfloor and the top of the joist. If you
use a flashlight and run the beam up against the
bottom of the subfloor, you will easily see the spaces
that need wedging.

If the subfloor is tight on the joists, it means that
the finish floor, or underlayment in kitchens, is rising
and falling as you walk on the area. Have someone
walk on the floor, and see if you can localize the loose
area by listening for squeaks from underneath in the
basement. Then drill several holes up through the
subfloor and partway into the finish floor. Drive home
several wood screws in these holes, and you should
pull the finish floor down tight against the subfloor,
eliminating the squeak.

If you can't get at the underside of the floor—as

when the problem is on the second floor—you'll have to find the loose spots and nail the floorboards down tight with special flooring nails that you can buy in a lumberyard. These have a barbed shank so they hold very tightly once driven into the wood. Try to get not only into the subfloor, but also into the joist underneath. Sink the heads of the nails below the surface of the floor by using another nail as a nail set. Then fill the hole with wood filler from a tube.

Squeaks caused by bridging members that rub are solved with your saw. Run the blade where they touch, and you will get a clearance space the thickness of your saw blade. That's all you need do to eliminate the rubbing for good. While you're at it, hammer tightly any loose nails in the bridging.

Other Kinds of Damage

Extensive repairs, such as removing split hardwood flooring boards and replacing them, should probably be left to the experts. But you can repair lesser dam-

Screws can be driven through the subflooring and into the finish floor to eliminate another cause of squeaks.

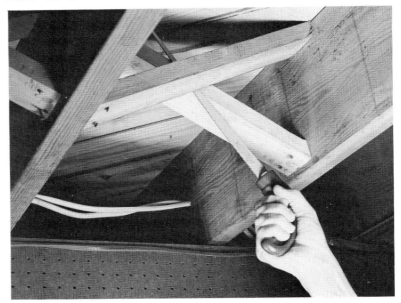

Run your saw between the bridging members to make sure they don't rub.

age yourself. Gouges and dents, if they are small, can often be lifted with the wet-rag and hot-iron technique. With a sharp knife, scrape off the finish from the area you want to raise before you try steaming the wood. This will permit the steam to penetrate the wood and make it swell up level with the floor. The spot will be a little rough after it dries, so you will have to smooth it with fine sandpaper or steel wool. Then finish with shellac or varnish from a spray can, and wax when thoroughly dry.

Larger cracks or gouges will have to be filled in with a paste wood filler that comes in a variety of colors. Don't try to match the color too closely with what comes from the tube or can. Rather, get a shade that you know will come out somewhat lighter. Then, when the crack or hole is filled, sand it smooth and use ordinary school crayons dipped in turpentine to blend in the color with the rest of the floor. A quick spray of shellac over the patch will make it nearly invisible.

Cigarette burns and similar tragedies can be treated in either of two ways. If the burn is superficial, use a single-edge razor blade to shave off the discolored wood and get down to the natural color of the wood. Finish and wax like any other repair described previously.

If the burn is deep, you'll have to sand the spot out. You can do this by hand, but it will take a long time. Floors are usually made of hard oak or pine, which are not the easiest woods to attack by hand. If you can rent or borrow a small power sander, you can make short work of the repair job. Again, after you get down to the bare wood, refinish the bare wood with a floor finish and wax.

Finally, when you wax floors, make sure you use a good product especially designed for floors and that you apply it in thin coats. A heavy coat will always look muddy, be hard to shine, and possibly hurt you by staying slippery in dangerous places like the head of a stair.

To apply a thin, even coat of wax quickly and easily, use the "old sock" trick. Put about a quarter of a cup of paste wax in the toe of a clean white gym sock. Twist the sock loosely a couple of times around this ball of wax and then put your hand in the top of the sock. This will permit you to cup the ball with the palm of your hand and rub it easily over floors or furniture. The heat of your hand will soften the wax, which comes through the end of the sock and is deposited in a thin, even layer wherever you rub. Best of all, you don't have to keep dipping a rag into a can of wax, leaving smears and lumps on the surface you are cleaning.

COMPOSITION FLOORS

Composition floors may be in the form of individual tiles of various materials, or in continuous sheets such as linoleum or sheet vinyl. Most of these floors require regular cleaning and waxing. Even the newer floors that need no waxing should be kept clean. No flooring material invented can resist the abrasion of sharp grit being ground into the floor with every step.

Water, together with a mild detergent, is recommended as the best all-round cleaner for these floors. Paste waxes can be used on all types of composition floors except asphalt tile. Nothing containing any petroleum solvent such as turpentine should ever be used on asphalt composition. Use a water-based or self-polishing wax on asphalt tile.

Unlike wood floors, a composition floor cannot be refinished. Once the floor is badly worn, it is taken up and replaced. Stains from foods, shoe polish, and other stubborn stain makers can usually be removed with ordinary household bleach, ammonia, or alcohol. Be careful of using any solvent on asphalt tiles; test a tiny corner first.

Damage to a composition floor will invariably consist of dents, gouges, or cracks. Cracks often occur when relatively brittle tile is laid over an uneven concrete floor. A little hump or ridge of concrete will eventually show through the tile and possibly cause it to crack along the line.

Repairing Tile Floors

Tile floors are easy to repair because you can remove the broken tile and replace it with a new one. The hard part comes in trying to match the tile. If you're on hand when the original floor is laid, try to put aside several spare tiles in a safe place for future emergencies. After some years, even this tile won't match perfectly with the already worn tiles, but it will be the best you can do.

Most tiles are installed with an adhesive that will soften under heat. You can warm the damaged tile with an electric iron or a heat lamp. As the adhesive loosens, pry up the tile with your scraper knife. Then clean the empty spot of all old adhesive with the scraper. Benzene can also be used to clean down to the bare surface.

Now, try fitting your replacement tile into the opening. If the tile is a trifle too big, trim an edge with a piece of sandpaper on a wood block. Test for fit frequently. Apply tile adhesive to the floor with your scraper knife, spreading it thin and even. Warm the replacement tile with your iron so it becomes slightly flexible, and then fit it into the opening. Step on all the corners, place some weights on it overnight, and next morning your repair is done.

If the tile cracked because of unevenness in the concrete underneath, you will have to fix that first; otherwise, you'll be repairing that tile over and over again for years to come. A small ridge of concrete should be hammered off, and any depressions remaining filled with patching plaster. The idea is simply to get a smooth surface, without ridges or holes, on which you will cement the replacement tile.

Patching Sheet Floors

Patching a hole in a sheet floor, such as linoleum or vinyl, can be done by you and your simple tools. The patch will be more or less visible depending on the pattern of the floor and how carefully you work on the repair. Basically, here are the steps in order:

1. Get a piece of patching material larger than the hole or worn spot you want to repair. (Steal a piece from under the refrigerator if need be.)

A damaged tile is easily removed with your scraper if you warm it with an iron.

Coat the floor or the back of the replacement tile very lightly with tile adhesive.

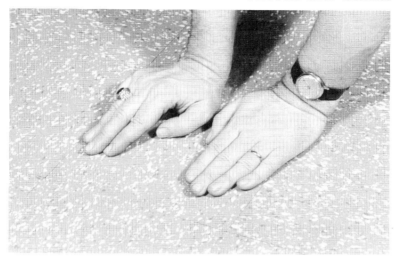

Warm the tile with the iron, and then press in place.

2. Fit this piece carefully over the defect and match the pattern as closely as possible. Then tape this patch to the floor with masking tape.

3. Get a sharp knife or a new single-edge razor blade and a straightedge.

4. Cut through *the patch and the original floor at the same time.* When you remove the patch and the damaged flooring material, the patch will be exactly the same size as the opening. Clean the opening with your scraper and a solvent like benzene.

5. Apply tile adhesive to the back of the patch, and fit it into place. Let it dry under a weight overnight.

You can make this patch almost invisible if you take pains to cut the patch along some line of the pattern that will hide the cut line. If the original floor is light without a prominent pattern, then you will have to accept the fact that the patch will show somewhat.

Slate and ceramic or quarry tile floors seldom need repair. If by chance one should crack under a blow, follow the same steps for repairing the damage as outlined for a composition tile floor. However, be prepared to do a lot more hammering to break out the pieces, because warming the tile with an iron is useless.

STAIRS

Stairs would probably be very near the top of any list of places where accidents happen most around the house. For this reason alone, you should take some time examining the various stairs in your home and doing whatever might be necessary to make them safer than the insurance companies' statistics.

In addition, because most inside stairs are made of wood, they share many of the same maintenance problems of your hardwood floors. In particular, wooden stairs can squeak worse than floors and be quite annoying with every trip up and down.

If you understand how stairs are constructed, many little problems will immediately suggest their own solution. The sides of the staircase that slope up from one level to another are called *stringers*. The steps are fitted in between them and consist of two parts: The horizontal part where you step is called the *tread*, while the vertical part is called a *riser*. Cellar stairs sometimes have no risers, but an open space between the treads.

Squeaking Stairs

Most squeaks on a staircase are caused by the tread and the riser rubbing against each other when you put your weight on the step. Eliminate the rubbing and the squeak goes, too. If the staircase is open in the back so you can see the back of the risers and the undersides of the treads, your job will be simplified.

Tighten all the wedges holding the steps in the stringers.

From under the staircase, look at how the steps are constructed. In most cases, the treads and risers are set into grooves cut into the sides of the stringers. Holding the treads and risers in these grooves are wooden wedges. If you give each of these wedges a sharp rap with your hammer, you'll tighten the whole staircase and eliminate squeaks. Another easy repair from the underside, in case the wedge treatment doesn't work completely, is to glue a number of small reinforcing blocks of wood to the inside corners formed by risers and treads. Use screws in addition to glue. The blocks reinforce the whole step and keep the two parts from rubbing.

If you can't get to the underside of your staircase, some other techniques must be used topside. One of the simplest which works in mild cases is to squirt some powdered graphite from a tube into the joint between riser and tread. It isn't permanent, but

Glue reinforcing blocks under the steps to eliminate squeaky stairs.

Some graphite lock lubricant in the joint between tread and riser will eliminate minor squeaks.

More serious squeaks require thin wedges in the joint. Coat the wedges with glue before driving.

squirting graphite once or twice a year is not a burdensome repair project.

More serious squeaks require some thin wooden wedges and glue for a cure. Look at the joint between riser and tread, and cut a number of wedges thin enough to fit in with just a little bit sticking out. Coat these thin wedges with glue, and hammer them tightly into the joints with your hammer and a block of wood. After the glue has dried, trim any exposed ends of the wedges with a sharp knife. Because they are so thin, you won't see them, and they can be covered the next time you paint the stairs. These wedges keep tread and riser from rubbing.

Stair Safety

The tread usually projects a little bit past the riser below and is rounded on the edge. This round edge is called the *nosing* and takes the worst beating. Metal

Trim the wedges flush with a sharp knife.

covers are available that you can screw over worn nosings to cover and protect them from wear. These metal nosings can be quite dangerous if they get loose. If you have them, or plan on installing them, make sure they are tight and flush against the nosing.

Pieces of carpeting or rubber treads are often used to cover worn steps. These too should always be installed with care; a loose corner can cause a nasty fall.

Handrails are another part of the stairs that should be checked from time to time. A handrail fastened to a wall can loosen in time; it is a simple matter to tighten up the screws. If the metal bracket holding the rail is loose because the screw holes in the wall are enlarged and won't grip, remove the bracket and replace it an inch above or below the original position.

More complicated wooden structures on the open side of a staircase are called *balustrades*. A balustrade consists of the handrail, the vertical posts supporting the handrail, or *balusters*, and the fancy main post at the beginning of the stairs called the *newel post*. If any of these pieces are loose in relation to each other, simple wedging with thin pieces of wood is all you need to firm up the whole balustrade.

Refinishing Stairs

Worn spots on stairs are refinished just like worn spots on hardwood floors—with one important exception. *Never* wax your treads, or you'll invite a serious accident. Risers, on the other hand, should be waxed to prevent marks from toe kicks as people walk up the stairs.

An ideal finish for stairs, in case you want to refinish them completely, is to use one of the special floor sealers available under various brands names. These sealers penetrate the wood and harden the fibers. If the finish wears, you simply wipe on more sealer later on and the match is perfect. After giving the treads two or three coats of sealer (as much as the wood will absorb) use fine steel wool to remove excess sealer from the surface. If you wish, a thin lemon-oil polish can be used on top of the sealer.

So much now for floors and stairs. Let's look at your walls.

Chapter 7

WALLS

WALLS REPRESENT THE LARGEST amount of surface area in your home. You have to paint them, decorate them, drape them with pictures and accessories, and, more than likely, repair them more often than other parts of your living area. Dents, cracks, gouges, and assorted injuries are much more visible on walls than on ceilings, for example, and call for more care in repairs.

Your simple tools, in most cases, are all you need to do quick professional repairs on all types of wall surfaces. Let's look for a moment at the different kinds of wall surfaces you may have in your home.

KINDS OF WALL SURFACES

In older homes, most of the walls are solid plaster. Even today, many people consider plaster walls superior to all other kinds, but increasing costs have driven most builders to adopt wall coverings that go up faster with less skilled labor.

Gypsum wallboard is used with increasing frequency in new construction and remodeling work. It consists of a gypsum plaster core between two sheets of heavy paper and comes in large panels in several thicknesses. The panels are nailed or glued to the studs that frame out walls or to the underside of ceiling joists to make a ceiling. Nail holes and joints between panels are covered with a special joint cement and paper wallboard tape. In a quality job, the nails and taped joints are invisible.

Especially for the more informal room, the wood panel has become an important type of wall covering. The cheapest panels are made of thin hardboard and have a printed surface that can be made to look like any kind of wood. The more expensive panels consist of real wood veneers on top of a less expensive base. All the panels have vertical grooves to suggest the appearance of separate planks and to make joints easier to hide. A joint looks just like another groove.

In some homes, you'll find walls of brick, stone, or ceramic tile. Brick and stone seldom need repair, while tile walls are handled just the same as tile in the bathroom.

The tools and supplies needed for wall repairs are simple and inexpensive. You will need some patching plaster or spackling compound for repairing small cracks in plaster walls. For wallboard, you should buy some special wallboard joint cement; this comes pre-mixed in a can, or you can buy a bag and mix it as required with some water. The wallboard tape comes in rolls. You can also buy a small bag of joint cement and a roll of tape together in a single package.

The only tools you'll need will be your 4-inch scraper and something with a sharp point—the beer-can opener suggested previously is ideal.

PLASTER

Cracks in plaster walls are nothing to get alarmed about, unless they are so big you suspect the house is falling apart. Tiny cracks are virtually unavoidable as a house settles or as the plaster shrinks over a period of time. Cracks are particularly noticeable at the corners of doorways and windows.

Plaster Repairs

Hairline cracks should be repaired as follows. Clean out the crack with something sharp. Blow away the dust, or use a small stiff brush that you can work into the crack. Take a dab of the premixed spackling compound, or mix up a small amount to the consistency of soft dough, and press as much as you can in the crack with the tips of you fingers.

Your hands will work better than any tools. Wipe off the excess patching compound and let it dry thoroughly. Later, sand it flush and give the patch a thin coat of sealer or shellac before you paint over the repair.

Larger cracks require a bit more preparation. Use the can opener to undercut the crack so the patch will ultimately hold itself in with a wedging action. Brush out the dust and plaster crumbles, and then wet the crack thoroughly. Apply the patching compound with your scraper knife, and level it flush with the surface of the wall. If you've done the job right, all you'll need is a little touch-up sanding and sealing before hiding the patch with a new paint job.

If the crack still shows, it means the patching compound has shrunk below the surface and shows up as an indentation. The solution is easy: After the first patch is dry and sanded, apply a second coat of patching material with your scraper knife. Large cracks and holes invariably need more than one coat to make the repair invisible.

Large holes are repaired very much like large cracks. Clean out all the old plaster and wet the surface thoroughly before applying the patching plaster. Figure on two or more coats of patching

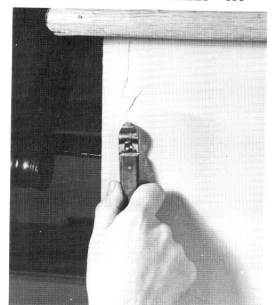

Clean plaster cracks with your can opener before filling.

Patching plaster is applied with the scraper knife.

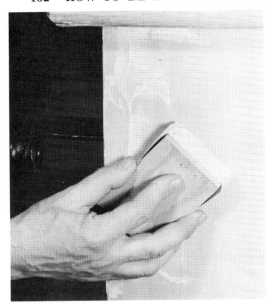

When dry, sand smooth with sandpaper and a block of wood.

material applied in layers to give a strong, smooth repair.

In a large hole, there must be something behind the plaster to give support to the patching material while it sets. If there is no wire or wood lath behind to give support to your patch, the simplest thing to use is a crumpled-up newspaper. Form it into a ball, and stuff it in the hole until it rests against the other side of the wall, with the front below the surface of the hole you want to patch. Wet the paper, especially around the edges of the hole, and apply a first coat of patching material to form a base for the subsequent coats of patching material.

After the final coat is dry, sand it flush with the surface of the walls, using a piece of sandpaper and a small block of wood. Then seal or shellac the patch before painting as with small repairs.

WALLBOARD

Wallboard is subject to the same kinds of damage that can be suffered by plaster walls, but in addition it can develop several other flaws or defects that you'll want to take care of to make your place look just perfect all the time.

Wallboard is nailed to studs and joists with special nails that have barbed shanks to improve their holding power. Even so, the nails will sometimes loosen and pop above the surface, revealing themselves as ugly little black circles. In addition, the taped joints can crack, or the edges can come loose. Fortunately, your 4-inch scraper, plus some inexpensive joint compound and paper tape, is all you need to make expert repairs.

Wallboard Repairs

Popped Nailheads If a nail pops through, try to remove it completely with the claw of your hammer. Usually, if it has loosened above the surface, it's loose enough to pull out quite easily. Use the same nail if it's straight, and nail it back into the wallboard an inch above or below the original hole. Here's the one point about wallboard repair that requires a little skill: The final blow of your hammer should drive the nailhead below the surface of the wallboard without tearing the paper surface.

In effect, you create a shallow dimple with the nailhead sitting in the middle of the depression. Put a bit of joint compound or spackling compound from a can on the edge of your scraper, and fill the hole. Use the edge to make the patch flush with the surface, and the ugly defect is completely hidden. Later, when the joint compound is dry, sand it flush, seal and paint just as you would for plaster cracks.

If the workmen who originally installed the wallboard were less than careful, you may notice quite a few depressions on your walls where the dimples were not finished flush with the surface. Before you repaint the walls, you should spend a few minutes giving each of these tiny saucers a skim coat of joint compound. Hold a flashlight against the wall and let the beam shine parallel to the surface and all the imperfections will stand out sharply in the form of highlights and shadows. Mark these imperfections with ordinary chalk, and then handle all the repair work at one time before redecorating.

Dents and Gouges in Wallboard   These are handled very much like the dimple repair. However, gouges and dents often tear or crush the surface of the wallboard so that the edges of the paper stand up above the surface. The little fibers will prevent a neat repair unless you get rid of them by first sanding the edges of the damaged area. After sanding, handle the repair as we explained before.

Repairing Holes   Small holes are handled like dents or gouges. If the hole goes all the way through the wallboard, chances are you will need several coats of patching compound to make the repair invisible.

Large holes are caused by accidents. It's not unusual to have a doorknob punch a hole in wallboard if a door is flung open sharply and there's no doorstop near the base to absorb the shock. Even if the damaged area is big enough for you to put your head inside the wall, don't despair; an invisible repair is possible and will clinch your reputation as a fix-it genius. All it takes is a little time. Here's what to do, step by step:

1. Get a piece of wallboard the same thickness as your present wall. Remember what we said about scrounging for scraps a while back.

2. With the fine blade of your turret saw, cut a neat square of wallboard large enough to cover

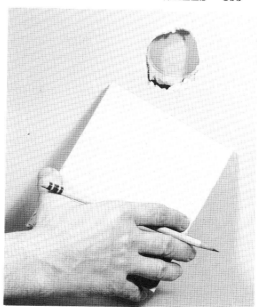

Cut a patch an inch or two larger all around than the area to be repaired. This is the finished patch.

Center the patch over the hole, and trace the outline.

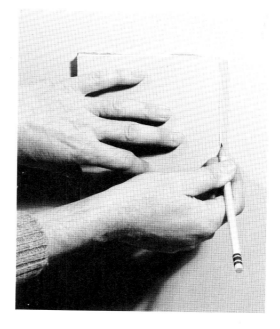

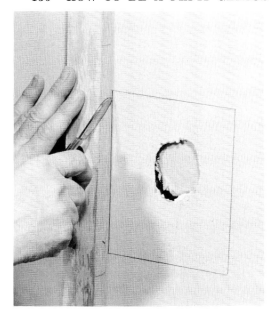

With a straightedge and a sharp knife, cut through the paper along the marked lines.

Saw out the square opening. An easy way is to cut to the corners from the center as shown here.

A sharp snap will crack the gypsum board along the scored lines.

Cut a patch larger than the hole. Coat the edges with joint cement, and using a hole in the middle as a finger-hold, work it in back of the opening and fasten tem-porarily with ordinary screws. This patch will provide a base for the finished patch.

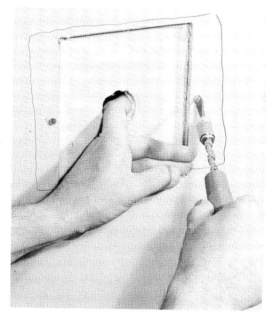

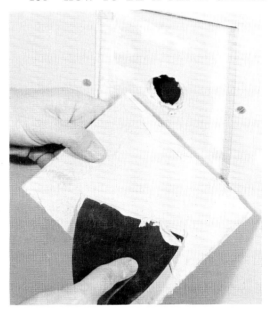

Coat the back of the finish
ed patch with joint cement
in a thin, even layer.

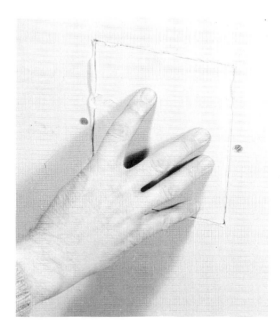

Press into place. Joint
cement should ooze around
the edges.

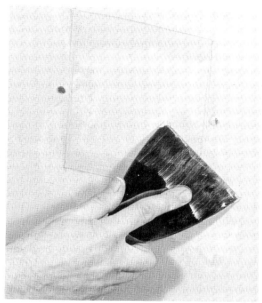

Level the joints with your scraper. Remove the screws later, and fill the holes with cement to complete the repair. Shellac the joints before painting over the repaired area.

the hole. Don't skimp—make the patch at least an inch or two larger than the hole all around.

3. Cut another piece of wallboard a little larger than the first, only you don't have to be too fussy with the edges.

4. Using the first piece of wallboard as a template, trace the outline of the board around the hole you want to patch.

5. Cut a neat hole with a knife and your turret saw. Follow the illustrated steps shown here.

6. Make a finger hole in the middle of the second piece of wallboard, and coat the border like a frame with joint cement.

7. Work this piece of wallboard in back of the hole, and pull it tight against the back of the wallboard making up your wall. Use a couple of screws to hold this piece of board in place while the joint cement dries.

8. Coat the edges and the back of the first patch you cut out with joint cement; then fit it neatly in place. Remove the screws.

9. Finish by filling the thin cracks around the patch and the screw holes with joint cement (two coats will probably be necessary), and then sand flush with the wall. Your patch will defy detection one it's painted over.

Here are some pointers we learned the hard way: Before you fill the cracks with joint cement, make sure you've sanded away every last trace of paper fibers sticking up from the cut edge of the wallboard. Secondly, don't worry if you can't seem to get the joint compound flush with the surface of the crack the first time. The more you press in the compound with your scraper knife, the more it seems to puff up like an angry vein. Let the bead of joint cement dry like that; after it's dry, sand it smooth and give a skim finishing coat.

The last hint we got from our legendary Scandinavian carpenter: For a really smooth job of feathering out the patch, sand with a wooden block supporting the sandpaper. Then take a moist sponge, not dripping wet, and wipe the edges of the patch smooth. The joint compound is water-soluble, and the moist sponge wipes the edges of the patch to microscopic smoothness.

Installing a New Wallboard Panel

You should know how to install a complete panel for several reasons. Major damage can often be repaired most easily simply by replacing an entire panel. Such damage is usually caused by water. Or you may want to cover up an opening in a wall, or even frame out a new partition and install a wall yourself. In any case, the job can be handled by you and your few tools.

The first thing you have to do is to remove the damaged panel. Punch a hole in it and give it a hard yank. This should loosen some of the nails and also show you where the panel is taped to an adjoining sound panel.

Step by step, do the following:

1. With a sharp knife slit the tape along the joints abutting sound panels.

2. Pull out the nails holding the damaged panel with the claw of your hammer. Don't be dismayed that this part of the job becomes a bit messy as the panel begins to crack and come off in pieces.

3. Tear off as much as you can of the tape left on the edges of the sound panels, and then sand smooth.

4. Get a panel of the same thickness as the original, and position it in place.

5. Use special wallboard nails, and nail the panel to all the studs. Nails should be about 8 inches apart, and the heads should be dimpled as we explained before.

6. Apply a thick layer of joint compound over the joint. The edges of panels are tapered slightly, and the compound should completely fill in this depression.

7. Press the paper tape into this channel of compound, and squeeze it along the whole length of the joint with your scraper knife. Once you try it, you'll discover the right technique of handling the scraper much more easily than by reading any description we may give.

8. Smooth the excess compound over the tape and let it dry. Sand thoroughly and apply a second coat of compound, feathering the joint

The first step when installing new gypsum panels is to cover the joints with a layer of joint cement.

> beyond the edges of the first layer of compound.
>
> 9. In extreme cases you may have to sand and give a third coat of compound. Either way, the last coat is sanded and sponged to make an invisible joint.
>
> 10. Cover all the nailholes, following the method use to eliminate popped nails described previously.

Gypsum wallboard is one of the most versatile materials to work with if you want to finish off unused space, build a closet, or even partition off an area like an attic into several rooms. The material is fairly inexpensive and can be painted, papered, tiled, or finished off in any number of ways. If you get ambitious after seeing how easy it is to handle, here are some additional hints you will find useful.

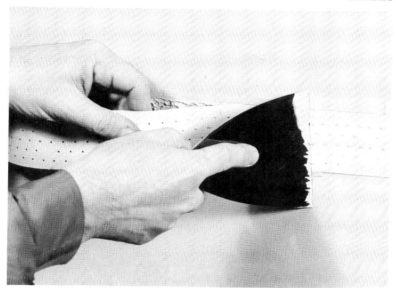

Use the scraper knife to press the paper joint tape into the cement. If the tape is perforated, the joint cement should ooze out of the holes. Smooth out lumps and ridges with the scraper.

When the joint is dry, apply another thin layer of cement and feather the edges into a neat, invisible joint. Sometimes a third feathering coat is used.

Straight cuts across the whole width or length of a panel are quick and easy if you use a knife and a straightedge rather than a saw. With a sharp knife, score the wallboard along a line you wish to cut. Then simply crack the panel by bending away from the cut. Separate the pieces by slitting the paper backing with the knife.

If you have an outlet box that will require an opening to be cut in the panel, you can locate the position very easily with this trick: Simply rub some colored chalk or crayon on the edges of the outlet box. Position the sheet where you want it; then rap it sharply with your fist in the area where you think the outlet box is. When you take away the sheet, you'll find a rough outline on the back of the panel where the chalk rubbed off and which you can use as a guide for cutting an opening.

Corners can be a little tricky. An inside corner joint must be taped just like a joint on a straight surface. However, you should fold the tape lengthwise before installing it in a bed of joint compound. With a little care, you can use your straight scraper knife to feather the compound on both halves of the tape. Some professional installers use a special corner knife, but you can easily get away with the simple tool you have.

Outside corners should be reinforced with metal corner beading. This is metal angle with a lot of holes all along its length. Nail the wallboard flush to an outside corner, and don't bother to tape the outside corner. Instead, cut the metal corner bead to the required length with the metal-cutting blade of your turret saw, and nail it on both sides of the corner. This gives the corner the reinforcement of a metal edge. Then fill the corner area with joint compound, and feather it away from the edge on both sides of the corner. You'll find that the metal bead on the angle automatically enables you to get a straight, smooth corner with a minimum of fuss and skill.

Finally, should you ever tackle a ceiling job, you'll discover that a whole panel can be very awkward and heavy if you try to handle it yourself. Get a strong helper to hold the panel at one end while you nail at the other end. After you have a few nails started, you can let go and start nailing toward your partner.

Repairing Split or Wrinkled Tape As your house settles, two or more of the wallboard panels may shift slightly in relation to one another. In such a case, the tape and compound that originally concealed a joint becomes apparent. An edge of the tape may lift up, or the panels may move toward each other so that the tape wrinlkes at the joint and shows itself as an unsightly raised seam. These repairs need both tape and compound. Here's what to do:

1. Lift up the damaged tape and remove it as far as it shows. Try not to go too far into the sound part of the taped joint.
2. Apply joint compound liberally over the whole damaged area.
3. With your scraper knife, press a suitable length of new tape into the compound, smoothing the excess over the tape very lightly.
4. When dry, give another thin coat of joint compound and feather the edges.
5. When this second coat is dry, sand with a block, using the wet-sponge trick we told you about. Result: an invisible professional repair.

WOOD PANELS

Years ago, real wood paneling was a luxury found only in wealthy homes. Today, veneered wood panels are one of the most good-looking and economical wall coverings available.

Basically, the wall panel is a sheet of relatively inexpensive plywood over which is glued a thin veneer of any one of scores of woods available for fine furniture. On very low-cost panels, this top veneer of real wood will be eliminated and a layer of printed wood or composition will be used instead. Modern technology makes such panels hard to distinguish from real wood because the grain is so well simulated.

The panels all have vertical score lines in a seemingly random pattern to suggest that the panel is made up of individual planks. Careful examination will reveal that a vertical score line appears at every multiple of 16 inches, even if other score lines appear anywhere within that space of 16 inches. If you recall that your walls are constructed of vertical wood members that are 16 inches apart, you will quickly see the reason for these score lines. The edge of each panel begins a vertical stud. Thereafter, a vertical score line falls over every other stud making up the wall. The score line serves several important purposes:

1. When several panels are butted together to form a continuous expanse of wall, the joint between the panels looks no more conspicuous than another score line.

2. The 16-inch multiples of certain score lines make it easy to install the panels; each time you nail, you can be sure of hitting a solid wood stud underneath the score.

3. Finally, the small nails holding the panel to the wall are easily hidden if nailing is confined inside the score lines.

Installing Wood Panels

Wood panel walls are used a lot in new construction because they look good, are easy to install, and are a lot less expensive than plaster or wallboard. If you plan on finishing off an attic or basement, you should certainly consider how easy the job could be made if you decide to use panel walls.

Wood panels are also amazingly versatile and easy to use in remodeling and redecorating projects. If you are repainting or papering a room, consider paneling one whole wall for contrast. For your first project, you should avoid a wall that has windows or too many complicated openings to work around. Here are the simple steps to follow.

1. Remove the existing wood moldings along the floor and ceiling if they exist.
2. Remove all electrical switch plates, outlet plates, and electrical fixtures installed on the wall you plan on paneling.
3. With the wood base molding removed, it is fairly easy to discover the location of the vertical studs in your walls. The molding is usually nailed directly into a stud in addition to the horizontal member called a *plate* that is fastened to the floor.
4. Start your paneling in one corner. Make sure that the other edge of the paneling falls over the center of a stud. If not, you'll have to measure from the starting edge to the stud and trim the panel to make the demensions come out.
5. Then all you do is use small finishing nails (four-penny nails, or about 1½ inches long), nailing about 8 or 10 inches apart up and down each score line that falls over a stud. You're sure this way that each nail is being driven home into the solid wood stud.

Cutouts for fixtures and openings are all done before nailing. Rub chalk or soft crayon on the edges of the exposed box after you've removed the covers and the switches and receptacles. (Make sure to turn off the current first!) Hold the panel in position and rap it sharply with your fist where the approximate location of the electrical box falls on the panel. When

you remove the panel, you should have a rough outline where the box is located. Then all you do is drill a
few holes at the corners and use the narrow keyhole
blade of your turret saw to make a neat square opening. When you fit the panel for nailing, the cutout
should fall exactly over the electrical box.

If you get ambitious and want to panel around
windows and doors, you'll get a much more profes-
sional-looking job if you first remove the trim around
such openings. You can then replace the trim on top
of the relatively thin paneling, or buy new trim in
woods that match the panel you've just installed.

Another way to install wood paneling, particularly
over old walls that are being redecorated, is by the
use of mastic or adhesives. The installation steps are
similar to nailing except that you don't have to worry
about lining up score lines with the center lines of
studs. After you've removed all moldings and made
all the necessary trim cuts and openings for outlets in
a panel, you fit it very close to the ceiling to make
sure everything fits. Remove the panel, and apply
dabs of mastic with your scraper knife on the wall
about a foot apart in each direction. Spread the mastic around with the blade so no large lumps stick up.

Then place the panel in position and nail it very
close to the top edge along the ceiling. Press the panel
in place, and then swing it out a few inches from the
wall to let the mastic get tacky. After a few minutes
you swing the panel back against the wall and tap it
home with your fist wrapped in a towel. The bottom
molding is replaced and you're done.

Whether you use nails or adhesive, you'll have a
few nailholes to touch up. The place that sells panels
invariably sells touch-up sticks. These look like over-
sized crayons and come in colors to match the particular panel you have chosen for your room. All you do
is rub the stick over the nailhole (set the nails slightly
by tapping them with another nail) until the hole is

filled up. Then wipe off the excess with a clean cloth and the nailhole will be practically invisible.

Maintenance and Repair of Wood Panels

If you accidentally punch a hole in a panel with a piece of heavy furniture, or make an unusually large scar, the best solution is to replace the whole panel. (Before attempting this repair, make sure you can still get a panel that matches; otherwise you'll have to replace the whole wall.) If you used nails to install the panel, removal is quite simple. All you do is drive the nails all the way through the panel with another large nail. When all nails have been punched through, the panel will fall off the wall quite easily. If you used mastic, then you have a problem. The panel will have to be scraped off the wall and the old mastic softened and removed with solvents.

Small dents can sometimes be removed with a wet rag and an electric iron. Wet the wood with the rag, and touch the spot with the tip of a hot iron through a

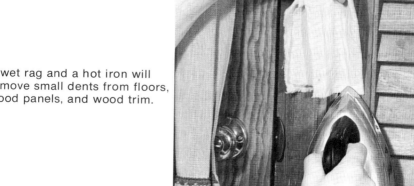

A wet rag and a hot iron will remove small dents from floors, wood panels, and wood trim.

wet corner of the rag. Make believe you're pressing a seam. The steam will cause the wood to swell and the dent to rise up level with the surface. Some fine steel wool and wax will make the spot virtually undetectable.

Scratches can be touched up with colored touch-up crayons or furniture polish. Before trying the repair on a spot that shows, test the color on a smaller scratch near the floor. Often, the dyes in furniture polish cause the scratch to darken considerably more than the surrounding wood. The answer is to use a lighter color, or just plain wax.

Once-a-year waxing is all that is needed on wood panels to keep them good-looking for years. Some panels have a plastic coating over a printed grain pattern. Here all that is necessary over the years is light dusting.

TILE WALLS

Grouting

The most common problem with tile walls occurs in the thin joints between the tiles. These joints are filled with a very fine white cement called *grout*. In time, the grout dries up and falls out, making it easy for water to get behind the tile and damage walls and ceilings below. Another common trouble spot is where the tile walls meet the top of the tub. Uneven expansion and contraction due to heat cause the grout to loosen and fall out. These repairs are very simple to handle, and you shouldn't let the problem persist beyond the first time you discover it.

Buy yourself a small box of grout in any hardware store. In addition to the grout you'll need a beer-can opener and an ordinary sponge from the kitchen. Here are the simple repair steps guaranteed to enhance your fix-it-genius reputation with others in the house:

Use the can opener and scraper knife to loosen and remove all the crumbling grout in joints.

1. Scrape out all the loose grout with the can opener. You can also use the edge of your scraper to get into tight joints.

2. Mix the grout with water according to directions. Then force it into the joints with your fingertips, the scraper, or the edge of a slightly dampened sponge. A little experimenting will show you which method works best for your particular repair.

3. Let the grout set for about 15 minutes. Then wipe off the excess with a damp sponge and your repair is done just the way a professional would do it.

Replacing Broken Tiles

Repairing a broken tile is a little more complicated but still within your capability. The first thing you have to do is to remove the broken tile without dam-

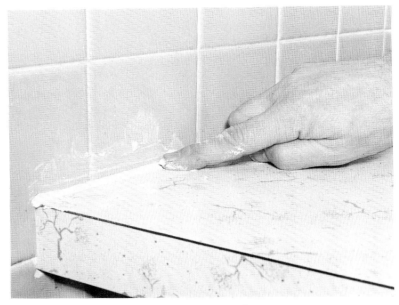

Press the grout into the joints with your fingers.

Use a wet sponge to smooth out the joints before the grout has begun to harden.

aging the rest of the tiles. Use the tip of your screw-driver or scraper to try and force the remaining pieces off the wall. Don't be surprised if you have to simply give up on prying and use your hammer to crack the tile into small bits for removal. Try to salvage a big piece so you will have something to take to the tile dealer for matching purposes. If the tile was originally installed with mastic, a solvent like lacquer thinner will sometimes soften the adhesive and let you get the tile off.

If the tile is impossible to match at a dealer's, see if you can steal a tile from someplace else where it doesn't show. Sometimes, you can pry off a tile carefully from behind the toilet bowl or under the sink where an unmatched repair tile won't be noticeable. This tile should be a perfect match for repair purposes because ceramic tile doesn't fade with age.

To replace the tile, do the following:

1. After removing the old or broken tile, clean out the area with your scraper and a solvent if necessary. Try the new tile in place, and make sure it doesn't stick up beyond the surface of the rest of the tiles. If it does, you'll have to clean deeper behind the repair spot.

2. Coat the back of the tile with a thin coat of mastic. Keep the mastic about ½ inch from the edges of the tile; you don't want the excess to squeeze up between the joints.

3. Press the tile in place, making sure the joints are about the same thickness around the four sides of the tile. Use bits of a matchbook cover to shim the tile evenly if necessary.

4. Press grout into the joints with your fingertips or a sponge. After about 15 minutes remove the shims and complete the grouting. Wipe off excess with a damp sponge, and the job is finished.

Broken soap dishes and towel holders are repaired much like broken tiles. You remove the old piece with hammering and prying. Get a replacement that fits the existing hole in the tile wall, and install it with grout or mastic. However, before grouting the joints, let the fixture dry overnight. Hold it in place with heavy masking tape. The next day you can grout the joints to complete the repair.

Waterproofing Joints

The joints between tubs and sink tops and walls are usually filled with grout. This is the easiest way to handle the joint, but the grout often needs replacement. A more permanent solution is to use one of the newer caulking compounds that were originally designed for sealing joints in spaceships. These compounds are available in convenient tubes and make neat, long-lasting repairs that are not affected by changes in temperature.

Chapter 8

CEILINGS

IT'S TIME TO look up now and consider your ceiling. Many years ago, ceilings were treated almost like large canvases on which were spread enduring works of art. The homes of the wealthy were lovingly decorated. Even until this century, ceilings were often embellished with ornate plaster carvings and intricate and hard-to-dust moldings. Then came a period when ceilings were made as plain and bare of detail as possible—an absolutely flat sea of white plaster.

Now we are returning to an era when ceilings are becoming more interesting in that a variety of coverings and treatments are available to dress up this part of the room.

If your ceiling shows a number of cracks or other defects, rather than patching them, you might consider redoing the whole ceiling in one of the newer tile or panel treatments. Suprisingly enough, redoing the whole ceiling can sometimes be easier than patching and will produce much more spectacular results when you're done.

SIMPLE CEILING REPAIRS

Most of the time, your ceiling will be made of the same material as your walls. Therefore, if you have holes, cracks, or popped nailheads, these defects should be handled exactly as described in the chapter on walls.

One flaw is quite common on ceilings, though less frequently seen on walls, and that is water damage. You need no description of water damage because it is so obvious. Less obvious is the cause. Before you do any repair work on the ceiling, the cause of the water damage must be found and corrected.

Don't make the mistake of thinking that the spot was caused by some freakish event that won't happen again. If there is a crack in a shingle or a split in your roof flashing, you can be sure it will cause you trouble again in the future.

If the leak was caused because someone was careless in the upstairs bathroom and let the shower leak past the tub onto the floor, then do something about the shower. You may need a new shower door or calking around the tub. The important point we wish to stress is that you discover and correct the source of the damage so your repair efforts won't have to be repeated at another time.

If your ceiling is gypsum wallboard with taped joints, it sometimes happens that the whole length of tape becomes visible because the panel has shifted slightly. You can fix this tape defect just as you would a similar fault on a wallboard wall. However, it is usually much more of a job because the defect will often stretch the length of the room.

Sometimes it's easier to hide it than fix it. One simple way to do this is to install false beams on the ceiling if the room decor can stand such an informal treatment. These beams are made of hollow wood or light plastic and are usually glued to the ceiling to give the effect of massive beams with plaster panels in between.

INSTALLING CEILING TILE

Somewhat more ambitious, but easy nevertheless, is the installation of a tiled ceiling. Most of the time, the existing ceiling is sound enough that you can merely glue the tiles on the ceiling with special ceiling mastic. In extreme cases where plaster is cracked and missing, or if you want to put up a tiled ceiling in a newly finished room, you might have to install strips of wood to hold the tiles. These strips are called *furring* strips and are nailed into joists and run at right angles to them. Then the tiles are stapled to this lattice of wood strips.

The first step is to choose the type of tile you want. The most common size is 12 inches square. The material may be plain or decorative; some tiles are acoustic.

Measure your room accurately, and make a diagram on paper to get an idea of the tile layout. It is highly unlikely that your room is of such even dimensions that you'll be able to install tiles without trimming them someplace. The trimmed tiles should run around the edges of the ceiling and be as even as possible all around.

Transfer your centerline to the ceiling with a piece of string rubbed with chalk; have a person hold each end tightly, while you snap the string sharply in the middle. You'll get a straight chalkline that you can use as a guide for starting the rows of tiles.

Tiles are glued to the ceiling with tile cement. Apply five dabs, each about the size of a walnut, on the back of a tile—one dab near each corner, plus one in the middle. Then you press it onto the ceiling and put a few staples in the lip of the tile with a staple gun you rent at the store that sold you the tiles.

Thereafter, as you glue the tiles on the ceiling, you slide each one into the matching groove on the previous tile, stapling the exposed lip as you go along. In a remarkably short time, if you don't stop too much to admire your progress, you'll have a dazzling new ceiling that can be the dramatic highspot of your home.

REPAIRING CEILING TILES

At the time you buy tiles for your ceiling, make sure you buy a few extra for later repairs. The ceiling tiles are made of soft, fibrous material. They are easily damaged by poking with sharp objects, such as might happen in a recreation room if you're careless with a pool cue.

Remove a damaged tile by cutting through the joints with a very sharp, thin knife or a single-edge razor blade. The idea is to cut off the lips that go into adjoining tiles. Then remove the tile by pulling it off the ceiling and cleaning off the old mastic. Take your repair tile and trim off the lips so the tile will fit into the opening. Apply mastic, press into place, and you're done.

SUSPENDED CEILINGS

A suspended ceiling is an easy way to change the character of a room, improve the lighting, cover ugly pipes, or hide broken plaster. A system of interlocking metal grids is first installed suspended a few inches from the old ceiling. Ceiling panels are inserted inside and simply lie on these grids, forming a good-looking modular ceiling.

Like tile, ceiling panels come in a variety of finishes. In addition, you can get clear and frosted plastic panels that form good-looking light panels when a fluorescent fixture is installed above them. Special fixtures are available that fix into the modular grids and take up very little space vertically.

Full instructions come with the particular grid system you purchase. In general, the installation steps are as follows:

1. You first nail an L-shaped metal angle all around the walls of the room at least 4 inches below the existing ceiling or the undersides of the ceiling joists.

2. On these angles you install the main T-shaped members. To prevent them from sagging, they are supported every few feet with a metal bracket you nail into the joist, or with a piece of wire that is wrapped around a screw eye that is

A suspended ceiling is the easiest way to hide pipes, ducts, or ceilings in poor condition. A hammer, saw, and pliers are all you need to do the installation yourself.

installed in the subflooring above and then through one of the many holes in the main T member.

3. Shorter cross T members are installed at right angles to the main T's by snapping them into holes in the T members. This finishes the metal grid system. Sight along the bottom edges, and if you see any sags, shorten the wires that hold the main T members at appropriate spots.

4. Install the ceiling panels by simply inserting them into the opening and then letting them lie on the lips forming the T on both main and cross members. It's as simple as that.

If a ceiling panel is damaged, all you do is replace it with another one. You don't even need any tools.

These few suggestions should go a long way toward making any room look new with a different ceiling. There is one final hint that occasionally is useful with a problem ceiling. If the ceiling is very high and has visible pipes or ducts, sometimes the easiest way to hide all this is to paint the ceiling and all the pipes a flat black. If light comes from fixtures below the level of the black paint, virtually nothing will be seen of the unsightly elements.

By now you should be capable of tackling the more annoying problems of doors, locks, and windows.

Chapter 9

DOORS

MOST PEOPLE TAKE DOORS for granted until something goes wrong. Considering the abuse that most doors endure, it is amazing that they work so well for so long. Doors, particularly outside doors, must function smoothly in all kinds of weather, fit tight to prevent drafts, provide security, and still look impressive as the first thing that a visitor sees upon entering your home.

It makes sense to examine all the doors in your home occasionally to prevent small problems from growing into large, professional-type repairs. Most of the time a little oil on the hinges, a squirt of graphite lubricant into the lock mechanism, and a tightening of screws in the strike plate and lockset will keep a door functioning without trouble for years.

UNDERSTANDING COMMON DOOR PROBLEMS

The most common problem with doors is difficulty in opening and shutting. If you take a moment to look at a door and how it is installed, you will easily see how such a problem can be caused and the commonsense steps to take to repair the annoyances.

The opening into which a door fits is framed out with wide pieces of wood called *jambs*. One-half of each hinge is fastened to a side jamb, while the other half is connected to the door. When closed, the door fits snugly up against thin strips of wood molding that form little ledges against which the door stops. These strips of wood are called *doorstops*. A lockset of one kind or another is fitted into the edge of the door, while a metal plate called a *strike plate* accepts the latch bolt which keeps the door shut.

On outer doors, the edges of the door and the doorstops are fitted with some type of weatherstripping to keep out drafts. This can be something as simple as a strip of felt that fits up against the door when it's shut, or it can be a fairly intricate system of interlocking metal strips and grooves that really need professional installation for best results.

Doors That Stick

If a door swells, or a hinge loosens, or even if the house settles slightly, the relationship between the shape of the door and the opening in which it fits is altered. It doesn't take more than a fraction of an inch one way or the other to cause binding and sticking. The first thing to check is where the door is binding, and to see if any of the hinges are loose. Look at the diagram and you'll see why a door will bind at top or bottom as a result of loose hinges or a shifting door frame. It is obvious, therefore, that:

1. *If a door binds at the top*, you should *tighten the top hinge* to bring that edge closer to the hinge side. Another cure is to add a small cardboard shim to the *bottom* hinge, which, in effect, will pivot the door so that the top moves slightly away from the jamb to cure the binding condition.

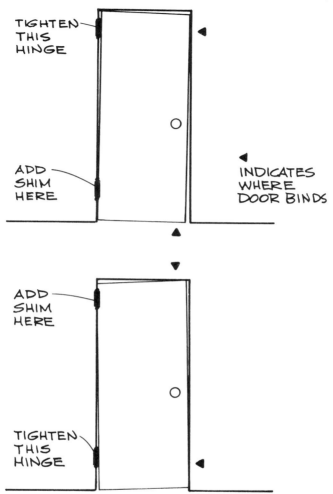

This diagram shows how shims under the proper hinge can cure a binding door.

2. *If a door binds at the bottom,* you should *tighten the bottom hinge* to bring that edge closer to the hinge side. Again, you can add a small cardboard shim to the *top* hinge, which will pivot the door slightly downward so that binding at the bottom is eliminated.

Tightening Hinges Put the biggest screwdriver bit you have in your ratchet screwdriver, and tighten the screws that hold both halves of the hinge to the door and the jamb. With wear, the screws will sometimes loosen and enlarge the holes so that it's impossible to tighten them. In such a case, you can solve the problem with a few old-fashioned wooden matches and some glue.

Remove the screws and the hinge. Put some glue on the wooden end of the match, and stuff it tightly into the old screw hole. You may need more than one match. Cut the matches flush with the top of the hole, and let dry. Put the hinge back, and you will find that the screws will now hold as tightly as if they were installed in new wood.

Installing Shims under Hinges Thin cardboard, no thicker than a shirt cardboard, makes an ideal shim to put under a hinge when fixing a sticky door. Remove the hinge, and cut a small rectangle of cardboard the same size as the mortise in which the hinge fits. Then simply replace the hinge on top of the shim. If it's too thin, add another piece of cardboard; if too thick, look for a thinner piece of stock.

Trimming Doors This can be a tricky job if any amount of wood has to be removed. Before deciding that a door is too big for the frame and must be trimmed, make sure that the problem can't be cured with a tightening of the hinges. If metal weatherstripping is used, it's quite possible that a portion may be bent and is causing the sticking problem and that the door doesn't need trimming. Run a stiff piece of paper along the weatherstripped edge with the door almost closed. This trick will help you find a place where the stripping is bent and causing the sticking problems. Use your pliers very carefully to straighten out bent parts of the metal.

You should confine trimming operations to only what can be accomplished with some coarse sand-

Cut a thin cardboard shim the same size as the hinge mortise, and then replace the hinge screws.

paper and a wooden block. Sawing and planing a door to fit perfectly is the kind of job they would give as a final exam in carpenter's school, so be wary.

Strike Plates

The little piece of flat metal with a square hole in it fastened to the door jamb is called a *strike plate*. If it gets loose and out of alignment with the latch bolt in the door, the door will not stay shut. If tightening the strike plate doesn't cure the problem, it's possible your door is slightly out of alignment and needs a shim under one of the hinges. If settlement has caused the strike plate to shift a little up or down, then you will have to reset the plate.

Remove the plate and notice how it fits into a little recess chiseled out of the jamb. Decide whether the strike plate needs to be raised or lowered. Then simply enlarge the recess with a sharp knife in that direction, and reset the strike plate. Because the screw holes won't line up now, you will have to fill them up with matchsticks and glue before putting back the plate.

Resetting Doorstops

If a door binds against the doorstop, it means the molding is too close to the door on the hinge side. Carefully pry up the stop molding with your hammer, and nail it back a trifle to give needed clearance as the door swings.

More common is too much space between the stop molding and the edge of the door. This is caused by the door's warping after installation and results in drafts and decreased effectiveness of any weather stripping. Again, pry up the molding and nail it closer to the door. One word of caution: Don't nail it too tightly against the door or you'll find that the latch bolt won't engage the strike plate and hold the door shut without a hard slam. A door should close easily with a satisfying sound of metal clicking into metal as on a luxury automobile. When closed, the door should not move any appreciable amount.

Warped Doors

Warping, especially of exterior doors, is caused by moisture entering the door. Prevention is always easier than the cure. Every door should be sealed, with either paint or varnish, *all over*. Most painters skip the most important part—the lower edge. This edge is exposed to moisture every time it rains, and eventually the door soaks up water and warps. The door must be taken off the hinges and the bottom edge completely sealed to prevent this entry of moisture. One careful builder we know carries a little mirror which he slips under the doors to make sure the painters don't skip this part of the job because it is impossible to see and a nuisance to perform.

Straighten a warped door by waiting for a dry, sunny day. Remove the door, and set it up on boards with weights in appropriate spots to counteract the warp of the wood. Do this on the lawn in the sun. Then hose down the door all over; if moisture can warp a door, it can also straighten a door. Let the door dry thoroughly, and with luck the warp will be cured. If the door resists this cure, you should consider a new door; the condition won't get any better.

LOCK PROBLEMS

There are several types of locks in common use, and it would take a locksmith to solve all the problems that can arise. However, as an amateur, there are several important and easy repairs you can handle:

Rim Locks These are sometimes called *night locks*. They are mounted on the rim of a door, usually in conjunction with a lock built into the door. About the only thing that can go wrong with them that you can fix is for the cylinder to become loose, thereby inviting entry. Remove the outer lockcase by removing the screws holding it in place. This will expose a mounting plate with a couple of long screws that go through the door and hold the cylinder tight up against the outside of the door. Tighten these screws and replace the lockcase. A little graphite lubricant before you cover the mechanism won't hurt, either.

Mortise Locks These are usually found in older installations. The lock is a sqare, boxlike mechanism that fits into a deep mortise cut into the edge of the door. Because of the design, it can collect dirt and eventually stop functioning. The solution is to remove the screws holding the lock in the door and lift out the whole assembly. Soak it in kerosene to remove dried oil and dirt; spray with graphite and replace. If a part is broken, try to replace the lock with a more modern cylinder lock. This will require boring a large hole in the door with a lock bit, which you can usually rent at the store that sells locks.

Cylinder Locks   These are of two types: a lightweight version without a key lock for use on interior doors, and a heavier version that accepts a key for use on outside doors. Any malfunctioning is usually caused by a worn or broken part. If the part can't be repaired, the whole lock will have to be replaced. Remove the lock by first removing the knob on the inside of the door. A little spring on the side of the knob is pushed in, and the knob slides off. Remove the long screws that hold the two halves of the lock together through the door. The simplest thing at this point is to take the whole assembly to the hardware store and buy a replacement that will fit in the existing holes.

Other Lock Problems

A stuck bolt is a frequent and annoying happening. A bit of graphite will cause it to move freely if lubrication is the problem. Otherwise, you'll probably find that paint was allowed to get on the bolt and is the reason for the binding. Solution: Scrape off the paint from the bolt. If these steps don't solve the problem, then you probably have a broken spring inside the lock that should be fixed.

A broken key can sometimes be removed by taking the lock from the door, turning it upside down, and rapping it sharply. A long thin needle is used to loosen the broken piece to make it fall out.

On a door exposed to weather, the lock will sometimes freeze during a sleety rain. If you're inside, all you have to do is put the tip of a fairly warm iron against the cylinder. Most often, though, you'll probably be outside trying to get in. Put the key in as far as you can without jamming it. Then warm the key with a match or cigarette lighter, and push it in further. By the time it's all the way in, the ice inside should be melted and the key will turn.

A binding key may be caused by a cylinder which

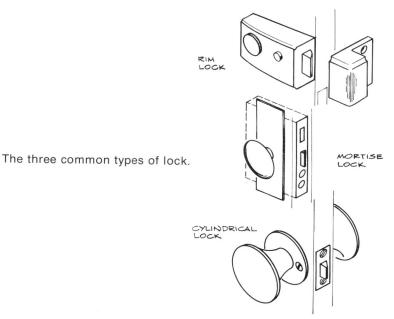

RIM
LOCK

MORTISE
LOCK

The three common types of lock.

CYLINDRICAL
LOCK

has loosened and turned somewhat. Loosen the lock, and try resetting the cylinder to the correct position where the key will work. If you're using a duplicate key, it may be a poor match, or a bit of metal burr along the edge of the key is causing the problem. Use a nail file on the burr.

OTHER DOOR PROJECTS

For appearance and security you may wish to replace glass panels with wood panels. Remove the glass by first removing the molding that holds the pane in place. Using the glass as a pattern, cut some thin hardboard or plywood the same size as the glass and install the panel in the door. Paint the whole door, and you have a changed front entrance.

Some doors, because of the kind of traffic using them, get a lot of wear along the bottom 6 inches. This is particularly true with swinging doors between kitchens and dining rooms; people kick them because their hands are often filled. The solution to this problem is to install a metal kickplate on the bottom of such doors. It's as simple a job as you could want, but the results are far out of proportion to your effort.

BURGLARPROOFING A DOOR

Nothing you can do will keep out a really determined intruder. However, a burglar is lazy like anyone else and will avoid entering a "difficult" place if an easier location is available. Therefore, you can achieve a great deal of protection, not by trying to make your entry impregnable (which is impossible), but in making it tough to enter so as to discourage the intruder. One of the best ways to make entry difficult is by installing an additional lock. This is the most common use to which a rim lock is put—as an adjunct to an already existing locking system.

You would be amazed at how often people will be careful to lock doors securely and go away with peace of mind, not realizing that a glass panel is close enough to the door that a burglar can bump out the glass with an elbow, reach in, and open the door. You can replace your present lock with a lock that needs a key to open it from both inside and outside, which will make opening the door difficult even with a hand inside the house. Or you can replace the glass panels with something sturdier.

Finally, if your door is made of thin panels, an intruder can punch in a panel with little trouble and gain entry that way. This mode of entry can be discouraged by reinforcing the door with an additional panel.

Close the door and make a light pencil line around three sides on the outside, using the stop molding as a guide. Open the door and measure the distance between the lines on the sides, and the distance from the line at the top to the extreme bottom edge of the door. Take these measurements to a lumberyard, and have them cut a piece of tempered hardboard at least ¼ inch thick to the exact size you measured.

When you get the panel home, roughen the door surface with sandpaper and remove all the locks. Brush glue all over the surface of the door, and glue the panel in the space outlined by the pencil marks. Use screws at intervals to keep the panel in place; after the glue has dried, even if the screws were removed, the panel would be impossible to remove.

Use your thin keyhole blade in the turret saw to cut out circles where the locks go, using the existing holes as a kind of template to guide the saw blade. Then replace the locks and paint the door. This solution to a big problem is likely to be cheaper and more effective than buying a third lock to put on the door.

Chapter 10

SIMPLE SOLUTIONS FOR MOST PLUMBING PROBLEMS

IF YOU'RE LIKE MOST PEOPLE, you treat the plumbing system with a fair amount of disinterest. After all, when you turn on the faucet the water is there; pull the plug and it goes away. What could be more simple? It's only when the water isn't there, doesn't go away, or suddenly appears where it shouldn't be that serious interest is aroused.

Probably most of your disinterest stems from the undeserved notion that plumbing is highly complicated and difficult to handle. This can be true for the plumber who installs the pipe, valves, and fixtures; but from a basic repair point of view, plumbing is really quite simple. At best, you can stop any leak in the house with a twist of a valve. And with only a few of your seven tools, you can solve some of the most annoying plumbing problems.

It's hard to tell in advance just when you're going to have a plumbing problem. You always know when the house needs a coat of paint, or when it's necessary to seal a crack in the basement wall. But plumbing systems seldom give any warning when trouble is brewing. Plumbing does deteriorate from the inside, where signs of trouble just can't be seen. And when problems arise, they often require immediate attention.

It is impossible to completely eliminate the possibility of plumbing problems, but there are many steps you can take to get much more mileage out of a plumbing system and to greatly extend the time between repairs. But before we go into this preventative maintenance, and the solutions to specific problems, it would be wise to get a basic understanding of the plumbing system. Knowing how it operates will make it much easier for you to work on it.

HOW THE HOME PLUMBING SYSTEM WORKS

Although your cellar and walls may seem to be crammed with pipe, valves, and tubing, the plumbing system is actually very simple. Basically, it can be divided into two parts—one system brings in the water, and another takes it away. If you have city water, it is pumped to your house from a central location and usually arrives at about 40 pounds of pressure. A well and pump system operates in the same way, except that your house is usually the only customer. When you open a valve, the pressure forces the water out. It's as simple as that.

The other part of the system handles the removal of the used water and is called the *drain* or *waste system*. Water coming from the water company (or well pump) arrives in small pipes, usually ⅜ to 1 inch in diameter. Water leaving the house flows in much larger pipes, varying in diameter from 1¼ to about 4 inches. There are several reasons for the need for this larger pipe size. Consider what would happen if every tub and fixture in the house were to be drained at the same time. The total diameter of the drain line would have to be large enough to carry away all the water.

And secondly, the drain system is open to atmosphere and not under pressure. The waste water leaving your house runs away; it is not forced as it is when it arrives from the water source. So, to prevent the creation of a vacuum and the restriction of waste flow, every home system is vented to the outside, usually through a pipe on the roof. The roof location ensures that the smells and gases of the flowing sewer will be blown away before they can become offensive.

Every sink, tub, and toilet has a bent pipe called a *trap* in the drain. Because this trap always remains filled with water, it acts as a barrier, preventing the odors and gases from entering the home. And believe it or not, it also prevents rats, which sometime live in sewer lines, from entering the house.

From a practical point of view, drain systems seldom cause leaks because they are not under pressure. But they do clog, and if the blockage is complete, there will be an overflow.

HOW TO SOLVE PROBLEMS IN THE WATER DELIVERY SYSTEM

Shutoff Valves

Find the Main Water Shutoff Valve Like knowing the location of all fire exits, knowing the location of the main water shutoff valve is very important. It is the first valve the water hits as it enters the house. So look for the point where the water line comes through the cellar wall and you will find it immediately. Often the water meter is installed between two valves, one on the inlet side and the other on the side leading from the meter to the fixtures in the house. Either valve can serve as the shutoff valve. Mark it clearly so that anyone can go right to it in an emergency.

Find the Other Shutoff Valves   The main shutoff valve will stop the flow of water to all parts of the house, but it is seldom necessary to use it. Most fixtures have shutoff valves (often called *supply stops*) located on the pipes where water enters the fixture. Look under a wall-mounted bathroom sink and you will find two valves, one controlling hot and the other cold water. You will find a single cold-water valve under a toilet tank. Bathtub fixtures may or may not have supply stops depending on access space. When repairs are necessary on such fixtures, you don't have to close the main valve; these remote shutoff valves will do the job. But remember, these valves can develop leaks too, and should be inspected regularly. When they do need repair, the main valve will have to be used to close down the water system.

Let's start where the water enters the house and cover the repair of each possible leak.

Leaks

Water-Meter Leaks   This is a real emergency. When the water meter starts leaking, the only thing to do is call the water company or a plumber—and do it quickly.

Fixing Valves That Leak around the Stem   There are a number of valves that are seldom used. The shutoff valve to an outside faucet and the shutoff valves behind tubs and under sinks and toilets are good examples. Because they are infrequently used, internal leakage around a washer is a rare problem with them. However, these valves will often develop leaks where the stem enters the valve at a part called the *bonnet* or *packing nut*. Regular faucets will also develop the same problem.

In many cases, it is possible to stop a stem leak without any difficult work. Because the stem is sealed against the water by a packing material under

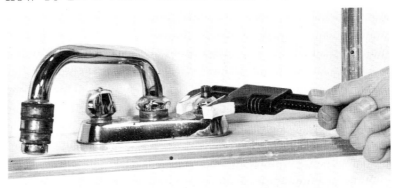

After removing the handle, you can stop leaks around the stem by tightening the packing nut. If the fixture is liable to be scratched, put some adhesive tape over the jaws of the wrench.

compression in the bonnet or packing nut, it is often possible to stop the leak—for a while—by simply taking up a quarter of a turn on the packing nut with the monkey wrench. This will pull the nut down, pressing the packing tighter against the stem and stopping the leak. Of course, the procedure must be repeated when the valve again leaks, and there will be a point at which it can no longer be done. Don't feel that this procedure is unprofessional. Valves are designed so that this adjustment can be made.

Of course, when this procedure no longer stops the trickle of water from around the stem, it will then be necessary to replace the packing. To do this, you will have to shut off the water that feeds the valve. If the valve is a faucet in a sink or tub, simply turn off the supply stop in the same line near the fixture. But if it is the supply stop, it will be necessary to turn off the main shutoff valve.

If the valve which is leaking is the main shutoff valve, don't monkey with it. Call the plumber. He will have to turn off the water outside the house with a special tool.

If tightening the packing nut does not stop the leak, remove the nut and replace the packing. Packing comes in the form of string; a couple of turns are usually sufficient.

To replace the packing, it is first necessary to remove the valve handle. Often this is quite simple, requiring only the removal of a small screw in the middle of the handle and a gentle tapping from below the handle. On faucets with decorative handles, it is sometimes necessary to either unsnap or unscrew a cap hiding the screw. When the handle has been removed, use the monkey wrench on the packing nut, turning it counterclockwise. If you are working on a plated valve in a sink or tub, place a layer of tape on the wrench jaws to prevent nicking the plating.

When the packing nut has been removed, use a screwdriver blade to pick out the old packing from the inside. Be sure that all the old packing is out before you go any further. You will need replacement packing at this point, and it is best to get some of the Teflon variety. This packing looks like heavy cord, and it is sold in hardware stores in precut, packaged lengths. The graphite-impregnated type of packing will work as well, but the Teflon types seem to wear and last longer.

Wrap enough packing on the stem of the valve so

that it will just fit comfortably under the packing nut. Cut the cord, and slide the packing nut in place. Tighten the packing nut snugly, and replace the valve handle. If the stem leaks after the water supply is turned back on, you have not tightened the nut sufficiently. Tighten the nut by a quarter turn at a time until the leak stops. New packing often makes the stem harder to turn than it was before. This is to be expected because the old packing had worn and was no longer doing its job.

There are some valves which do not use cord-type packing, but rather a formed disk or ring. This will be easily identified when you dig the packing out of the packing nut. When you encounter such packing, do not try to replace it with the cord type of packing. Rather, take the old packing, packing nut, and stem to a hardware store and buy a direct replacement.

Fixing a Dripping Faucet

Sink and tub faucets can develop a bothersome drip-drip-drip that is not only annoying in the middle of a sleepless night, but also very wasteful of water. This problem is easily solved with only the aid of your screwdriver and monkey wrench. You will also need replacement stem washers, the parts that wear in a valve and cause leaks. Because there are several sizes of washers, and you won't know which to buy until the valve is opened, we suggest that you buy a box of assorted replacement washers to keep on hand. If the kit of washers doesn't contain replacement screws, it is a good idea to buy a half dozen or so at the same time.

In concept, all home valves are essentially the same. A handle connected to a stem has a plastic or rubber stem washer attached to it. As the handle is turned, this washer is either lifted up from or screwed down on an opening leading to the pipe which supplies the water. As the stem washer is turned down on the valve seat, it will wear and become deformed. Eventually, it will wear enough so that it is no longer a good seal, and the valve will begin to drip. The longer you neglect the leak, the worse it will become. It's such an easy job to replace the washer that there really is no excuse for waiting—so let's get right to it.

Begin by first shutting off the water supply and then removing the valve handle. Some faucets have decorative handles which hide the head of the screw under caps which either snap on or are screwed in. Snap caps can be pried off with a screwdriver, and screw-on caps can be removed with your pliers. If the cap is decorative, place tape on the jaws of the pliers to prevent scratching.

When the handle has been removed, the packing nut should be removed. In some valves, this is a simple bonnet-type nut which is hollow underneath, and in others it is an assembly consisting of an outer housing, the packing nut, and the stem and stem washer.

When the valve is one using a simple bonnet-type packing nut, the next step after removal of the nut is to unscrew and remove the stem. This is done by simply turning the stem in the "open" direction until the stem slips out of the valve body.

The stem washer is held by a small brass machine screw in the middle. The normal shape of a good washer is conical, but a worn washer will often be flat and grooved. If the wear is even and smooth, you can replace the washer immediately by picking the correct size from your replacement pack. But if the washer appears to have been chewed up and is rough and shredded, the internal valve seat must be dressed or smoothed. There are special tools to do this job, but a satisfactory job can be done by rubbing emery cloth around the valve seat with a finger, smoothing off the burrs.

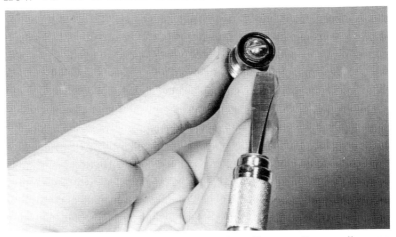

If the faucet still drips, replace the washer. Remove the small screw in the center of the stem, and put in a new washer.

When replacing the stem washer, first remove the brass screw and then dig the washer out with the screwdriver blade. Make sure that there are no pieces of the old washer left in the retainer before the new seat is installed. The new seat is installed with the cone shape facing out, and it should be held in place with a new brass screw.

Once the stem washer has been replaced, reassemble the valve by simply reversing the steps taken to disassemble it. Then open the supply stop, and check to see if your repair has worked. If, after you turn down tightly on the handle, there is still a trickle, it may be necessary to repeat the disassembly and apply the emery cloth to the seat again. If the seat is too badly worn or nicked, you may have to replace the entire valve.

The Slow-running Faucet

Over a period of a few months to a year, you may notice that a sink faucet begins to deliver water with less and less force. This occurs with faucets that have aerators attached to the delivery end of the valve. These aerators are filter assemblies which screw into the end of the valve and mix air with the water to give it that frothy look rather than a solid column of water. The aerator also contains a small filter screen which can be easily clogged by the tiny particles of mineral deposit that constantly appear in tap water.

To relieve this situation, simply unscrew the aerator, remove the filter screen, and clean it. However, a word of caution is important here. Some of these aerator assemblies have four or five parts. Note the order in which you disassemble the unit so that it can be reassembled in the proper order. Also, you will have to use your slip-joint pliers to remove the aerator. Be sure to put some tape on the plier jaws to prevent nicking the finish.

Leaking-Pipe Problems

A leaky pipe is an immediate problem, but is also a warning that more serious problems might exist. Occasionally a pipe will develop a pinhole leak that

A temporary repair of a small hole in a pipe can be accomplished with a piece of rubber and a pipe clamp. It's a good idea to have several sizes of pipe clamps among your emergency repair supplies.

can be temporarily stopped by wrapping it with plastic tape, but remember that this measure is strictly first aid. Two to three overlapped layers will be needed, and the outside of the pipe must be dry.

Another fast repair which is slightly more dependable is the use of an adjustable hose clamp to hold a piece of rubber over the leak. The rubber need be nothing more than a few pieces cut from a child's balloon. Four or five layered pieces will give sufficient thickness, but be sure to tighten the clamp only enough to stop the leak. Do not overtighten. If the pipe is badly corroded inside, this pressure could be enough to turn the trickle into a torrent.

Probably the most common pipe leaks develop where a pipe is joined to something else: an elbow, tee, valve, or any of the many different fittings used to complete a plumbing job. Often it is simply a matter of using the monkey wrench to give the pipe or the fitting a very slight turn to stop the leak. But remember that when you turn a pipe to tighten it at one end, you will be loosening it in some fitting at the other end. This slight turn may be just enough to stop the leak at the one end without causing a new leak at the other. It's worth a try.

Another way to handle leaks at joints is to apply one of the many epoxy materials to the leaky joint. In general, these materials must be applied to a dry, oil-free surface, so it will be necessary to turn off the water during the application and curing stages. Usually, the patch will benefit from a bit of pipe roughening with steel wool prior to this repair.

Commercial clamps are available at most hardware stores, but it really doesn't pay to buy them until a leak develops. And when they are bought, they should be bought with the idea that the repair is temporary. Little leaks are warnings of the possibility of more serious problems.

Up until now, we have been talking about pipe. To most people, everything that carries water is a pipe,

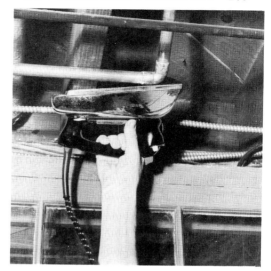

Water pipes near windows and other openings will sometimes freeze. Open the faucet served by that pipe, and then gently warm the pipe with hot water, a hair dryer, or even an iron.

but there is another line made of copper tube which is common today. Copper doesn't suffer from the same problems as steel pipe, but it is still possible to have a leak problem at a joint. These joints are soldered together, and the leaks usually result from either broken solder or a loosening of the soldered joint. This repair requires the attention of a plumber. He will drain the tube and, using a torch, will resweat (solder) the connection.

HANDLING PIPE FREEZE-UPS

A furnace fails during a winter vacation and the pipes freeze; a careless plumber installs a water pipe in an unheated crawl space and the first winter brings disaster. These and other conditions can present serious problems for the householder. If the line carrying the water is steel pipe, the expanding ice may actually crack the pipe. Copper is ductile, and when water freezes in the copper tube, a bulge is often noticeable. But however it happens, and in whatever kind of line, there is one thing to remember: Whatever method you use to melt the ice in the line, the heat must always be applied in a direction from an *opened* valve toward the freeze. The reason for this is simple: If the heat you apply raises the temperature to the boiling point, there must be an avenue of escape for the steam. If not, the steam can add to the pressure problems and cause a pipe which might not have burst to do so.

The simplest but often the longest way to unfreeze a pipe is to wrap the frozen part of the line with towels and to pour boiling water over them until the ice has been melted. A hand-held hair dryer can also be used, as can be a small room heater or even a electric iron. However, when using anything electrical, be sure not to put yourself in a position where the water pipe and appliance can result in a shock for you. Either use rubber gloves, or keep one hand in your pocket (as novice radio amateurs are told to do when first working with high voltage).

In any event, what we have just described is a way out of an immediate problem. A pipe in an unheated crawl space will freeze every time the temperature reaches 32° F, and you will have to do something about preventing that from happening. But this is not a job for you and your seven tools. It calls for a professional who can apply the best of the many methods at his command.

SOLVING TOILET-TANK PROBLEMS

Solving problems relating to the flush tank can be simplified considerably if you have an understanding of just how this system works. It isn't complicated at all. It just looks that way because the mechanism is always partially covered by water. Follow the drawing with this explanation, and you should have very little trouble solving flush-tank problems.

When the flush handle is turned, the trip lever in

the tank lifts the tank ball off its seat. This allows the water to rush from the tank into the bowl, flushing the contents into the drain line. Just as the tank is almost empty, the tank ball drops and closes the opening into the bowl and water begins to fill the tank. At the same time water is replaced in the bowl by means of a small loop of pipe called a filler tube.

As the water in the tank rises, the float ball comes

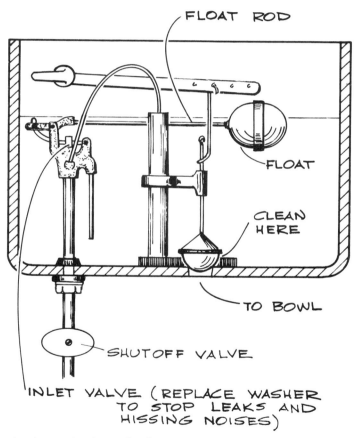

The basic mechanism of a flush toilet. When the toilet is flushed, the water level in the tank quickly drops. The float drops at the same time and opens a valve that begins the process of refilling the tank. As the tank fills, the ball rises and shuts off the valve. A lot of toilet ills can be solved by merely bending the rod holding the ball float.

up with the rising water level. When the level has reached a point just below the top of the overflow pipe, the float-ball arm closes a valve which seals the incoming water and the whole process comes to a stop, ready for the next flush.

There are only a few problems which can occur with the toilet tank, and each can be handled easily. Refer to the basic drawing as you read the solutions to the problems listed below. But in all cases, shut off the water supply to the toilet tank. If the tank doesn't have a supply valve, you must then turn off the main water supply valve.

Water Continues to Run in the Bowl and the Tank Doesn't Fill The tank ball is made of rubber. In time it will wear and must be replaced. Turn off the water supply and begin the repair by first flushing the tank. Remove the tank ball by simply unscrewing it from the thin rod. While the ball is out, clean the valve seat on which the tank ball rests. Do this by rubbing the entire seat perimeter lightly with a fine grade of steel wool. When the new tank ball has been positioned, check to make sure that the supporting rod rides upward freely through the rod guide. An application of the steel wool on this rod will remove some of the mineral scale which can cause a hang-up later on. Also check to make sure that the stem guide is in the proper position to assure that the tank ball will seat perfectly. If it isn't, simply loosen the locking screw and reposition the guide. Retighten the locking screw, and turn on the water supply. The tank will fill, and your toilet will be ready for use.

High or Low Tank Water Level The water level in the flush tank should be ¾ to 1 inch below the top of the overflow pipe. It is a simple matter to bend the float arm down a little to lower the level and upward to raise the level. However, don't grip the float ball itself when you make the bend. Use both hands on the float arm, or one hand and your pliers.

Tank Fills, but Water Continues to Run through the Overflow Pipe   First, check the position of the float ball as we have described above. If a slight downward bend in the float arm doesn't solve the problem, it might be that the float ball is leaking. Remove the ball from the arm by unscrewing it, and then shake it and listen for the sound of water. If water has begun to enter the float, there is no alternative—replace the ball.

If the ball is not leaking, and a downward bend in the float arm doesn't stop the filling process, there is one test which must be performed. With the tank filled (turn on the supply valve), lift the end of the float ball slightly. If this doesn't stop the flow of water into the tank, it will be necessary to check and repair the ball-cock assembly which delivers the water.

Before tackling the ball cock, shut off the supply valve and flush the toilet again. Then begin disassembling the ball-cock by removing the screws or pins which hold the float arm and valve assembly together. Everything, including the float mechanism and its linkage will come off at this point. Then lift out the valve stem and plunger, and examine the condition of the washer. This washer may be held in place with a brass screw, or it may be a press-fit. Either way, if it is worn or deformed, replace it. Many ball cock valves will have an additional seal, usually in the form of an O ring seated in a groove around the outside of the plunger. It is always a good idea to replace this ring at the same time. It is a secondary seal, but easy to replace while you have your hands in the tank.

While you're at it, make a thorough inspection of the entire ball-cock assembly. It will look pretty awful, usually covered with mineral scale, but this in itself seldom is cause for replacement. However, if any of the parts are worn to the point where they bend easily or break off in your hand, the entire mechanism must be replaced. Complete kits with detailed instructions for replacement are readily available in hardware stores.

SOLVING PROBLEMS IN THE WATER REMOVAL SYSTEM

Until now, we have been talking about the water delivery system only. All the repairs in this system are fairly critical because the water is under constant pressure. A small leak can become a large leak, which, if unattended, can flood your basement before too long. The drainage system is not under pressure, but under some circumstances can still produce a nasty flood.

Unclogging Sink and Tub Drains

Using the Plunger   All of the other six tools in your basic kit can be used for a variety of jobs, but the plunger has only one job to do. It is a very important job, which is not quite as simple as it might seem. The uninitiated might think that a simple up and down stroke is all that is needed to unclog a drain. Not so! But before we get into the details, you should understand what's happening in your drain line.

As we mentioned earlier, plumbing fixtures are connected to the main drain line by way of a U-shaped piece of pipe called a trap. Actually, there are other kinds of traps; the most common alternative, called a *drum trap,* is usually found in the tub drain line.

The function of the trap is to form a water barrier between the inside of the house and the outside sewer line, and to catch things which can clog a drain. These clogging things can be either accumulations of grease and hair or single objects such as toys which fall into the fixture. However, the most common cause of clogging is the gradual accumulation of junk which settles in the bottom of the trap. You can tell when the trap is clogging by the slower draining action. When the clog is complete, the water simply will not run off. Now is the time to use the plunger.

First of all, it is important that there be at least an inch or two of water in the bowl. The drain stopper must also be removed. If the problem is a complete clog, you've already got the water. But if you are trying to solve a slow-drain problem, place the plunger over the drain, and add an inch or two of water. It is also important that the overflow vent on the sink be covered. You can do this with a wet towel or with the palm of a hand. In the case of a dual laundry tub, the drain in the second tub must be plugged completely.

Now you are ready to use the plunger. Don't start by placing the plunger in an absolutely vertical position over the drain and plunging away. Begin by placing the edge of the plunger at the edge of the drain—but on an angle. This will keep most of the air out of the cup. Then push down firmly and straighten the handle, compressing the cup. Now—here's the critical point—pull up sharply. The cup will snap off the drain, and water will flow up from the drain back into the sink. Before this water has time to return down the drain, repeat the process. In other words, you are drawing the obstruction up, rather than forcing it into the main drain line. Get a little rhythm into this, and in less than a minute you should be able to clear the trap. Once the obstruction appears in the sink, cover the drain with the cup and remove the gunk from the bowl.

If you follow these simple steps, the old "plumber's friend" will do its job quickly, and it will not contribute to a further clog later on in the main line.

Using Chemicals to Unclog a Sink Drain   If the plunger fails, you might want to try one of the many chemicals developed for the job of drain cleaning. However, if the sink is full of water, it will be necessary to scoop out the water so that the chemical is prevented from contacting the porcelain surface of the sink and can get to the trap without being badly diluted. Pour in the amount of chemical stated on the label (this will differ with individual chemicals), and wait a few hours. If this step works, plenty of water should then be run through the sink to neutralize the chemical and to carry away the freed gunk. Never use a plunger until all such chemicals have been flushed away.

Probing the Drain with a Coat Hanger If the two previous steps fail, then straighten out a coat hanger and push it down the drain and into the trap. The hanger should be bent into a small hook at the end and used to withdraw the obstruction. The hanger should be pliable enough so that it will bend with the shape of the trap as it is forced down the drain. Twist the wire as it is pushed, and withdraw it after each few inches of penetration.

If you can't get it into the trap, the next best solution is to open the drain plug at the bottom of the U trap. Use a monkey wrench, but be sure that you have a bucket under the plug. If your U trap doesn't have a plug, the trap itself will have to be removed. Simply loosen the slip nuts at each end and slide the trap off. It is then an easy matter to poke in the trap and remove whatever obstruction is causing the problem.

Before the trap is replaced, check to see that the vertical line leading from the sink to the trap connection is clear. And it is a good idea to run your coat hanger into the horizontal pipe leading into the wall with a few vigorous thrusts and twists. When you are satisfied that these lines are clear, reassemble the trap and test the drain. If water still doesn't drain

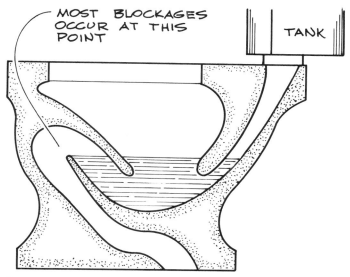

A toilet bowl has a trap built in. The plunger can be effective in dislodging small stoppages.

from the sink, the problem is in the main line, which is discussed later.

Unclogging Toilets

Basically, a toilet drain works the same as a sink, except that the trap is built in. A look at the drawing on this page shows how the toilet is laid out.

The first step to unclogging is to try the plunger. Use the quick pull-up stroke we have described for use with a sink to try to bring the obstruction back into the bowl where it can be removed. If this doesn't work, you can try putting your hand in a plastic garbage-pail liner and reaching back into the trap to pull out the obstruction. If neither of these attempts work, use the coat hanger and try to hook the obstruction and pull it back into the bowl.

If all these attempts fail, the best answer we can

Loosen the cleanout, and then force a garden hose as far as possible into the opening. Turn the hose on full force; be ready to shut it off quickly if this treatment doesn't work.

give is to call the plumber. He will probably have to get an auger bit into the obstruction to pull it out.

Unclogging the Main Drain

If water fails to drain and all the traps are clean, there just might be a blockage at the line leading from the house to the sewer. Open the cleanout plug, using your monkey wrench, but be sure to have a bucket handy to catch the trapped water. After this water has drained, run some water into each sink and tub in the house, and check at the cleanout port to see if this water runs quickly. If it does, the blockage is past the cleanout and is between the house and the sewer.

Many times it is possible to clean such blockage by simply forcing a garden hose down the drainline toward the sewer. It may not even be necessary to turn on the hose and use the water pressure. But if you do use water pressure, do it gingerly at first, to prevent back-flow and runout at the open cleanout plug. If the obstruction is close to the plug, use the coat hanger to either break it up or draw it out.

SOLVING OTHER PLUMBING-RELATED PROBLEMS

Fixing Wobbly Toilet Seats

A toilet seat is held in place by two bolts at the back of the bowl. Tightening the seat is simply a matter of using the monkey wrench to pull up on the loose nuts.

Replacing a Toilet Seat

When it comes time to replace a toilet seat, you will usually find that bathroom dampness has corroded the two bolts at the back of the seat to the point where they can no longer be turned with the wrench. Then, you must saw them off with the hacksaw blade of the turret saw. If you are unable to loosen the nuts enough to get the blade at the bolt, there is no other alternative but to saw through the nut and the bolt. This must be done with the blade pressed flat against the bottom of the base using great care not to damage the porcelain.

After removing the old seat, it is a good idea to give the bolts on the replacement seat a coat of oil or grease during assembly. This will slow down the corrosion that made it necessary to saw off the old bolts. You can also spray the snugged-up nuts with an acrylic material such as Krylon.

Preventing Pipe Banging

Water can't be compressed; and when the faucet is turned on, it flows like a ramrod through the pipe. If the valve is turned off quickly, you will often get a "bang" from the pipe. This condition, called water hammer, is not only annoying, it is dangerous because the force can blow open some connections.

Look in the basement for long, unsupported lengths of pipe. This pipe or tube should be attached to the cellar beams with small C-shaped clamps

Nail small clamps around pipes to prevent noise and vibration.

spaced about 6 feet apart. These clamps are available at any hardware store. Using the clamps may solve the problem, but if it continues, there is no other alternative than to call the plumber, who will install hydraulic "shock absorbers" in the line. These are air chambers which take up the force when the water is shut off quickly, eliminating the banging noise—and possible damage to the entire system.

Chapter 11

ELECTRICAL REPAIRS YOU CAN DO

IN A WORLD where so much work is done by electricity, it may seem odd that very little is known about electricity itself. We know how to make it, measure it, and use it, but it is a power which is still being studied by scientists. However, for the kind of repairs that you will do, the only knowledge you will need is that of safety.

Electricity is unique in that it is generated many miles from your home, transported by means of solid wire, then distributed to your house and converted to energy to do a wide variety of jobs. It can produce light, heat, and motion and can also be used to power a radio or television set. In a sense, the electrical system is somewhat like the plumbing system. There has to be a circuit—two wires—which delivers the current. When a circuit is completed (switched on), electricity flows from the power source, through the circuit, and back to the power source. The plumbing analogy holds only to the point of return. Water must leave the house, but it is not returned directly to the pumping station. It does get there again, though, through the diverse processes of nature.

UNDERSTANDING YOUR HOME ELECTRICAL LAYOUT

A look at the wire bringing power to your house will give you some important knowledge. If there are two wires coming in, your house is wired for 120 volts. In most cases, the two wires are insulated; that is, they are covered with a protective material. However, there are times when one of the wires may be uninsulated. This is the neutral line, but don't be fooled by the word "neutral"; it is very much a part of the circuit and it carries lethal voltage.

If there are three wires entering your house, it is wired for 240-volt service. One of the three is a neutral wire, but the voltage measured from either of the two "hot" wires will be 120 volts. Measured across the two hot wires, the potential is 240 volts. This high voltage is used only for heavy-duty appliances such as large air conditioners, electric ranges, clothes dryers, and similar equipment.

These wires go directly to a distribution panel where the incoming line is fused. It is here that the lines to the various rooms in the house are also fused. Fuses and circuit breakers protect your home and electrical appliances; they are discussed in detail in the section on fuses. It will be important for you to know which fuse or circuit breaker protects which outlet, light, and appliance. This will involve the drawing of an electrical "map" of your house; but before you undertake this step, you should understand all the safety precautions to take when working with anything electrical.

Electrical Safety

In the next few paragraphs, we will describe the safety precautions you *must* observe when doing electrical repair work. *If you have any questions at all—if there is any doubt in your mind whatsoever— play it safe and do not handle the repair yourself.* However, many of the repairs we describe are made on appliances which can be unplugged.

This, then, is the first rule of electrical safety: *When working on any electrical device which is not part of the permanent wiring system and which can be unplugged, be sure to pull the plug first.*

When making repairs to house wiring, such as outlets and switches, it is essential that the power be shut off. This means either removing a fuse completely or opening a circuit breaker. Don't make the mistake of thinking that because you have removed a fuse and the overhead light in the room went out, the wall outlet in the same room is also dead. Often, there are several circuits serving the same room, and each is on a separate fuse or circuit breaker. This is done so that there will be electrical power in the room in order to make repairs on other circuits.

To make sure that a circuit is dead, use an appliance such as a lamp in the circuit to be repaired, and remove fuses until the lamp goes out. If you're not entirely sure, pull the main fuse, circuit breaker, or main switch, and deenergize all the circuits. This process is described in the section on fuses.

If a circuit is energized, and you touch a bare wire while you are also touching another wire or something like a radiator or water pipe, current will flow through you and possibly kill you. Many houses have 100-ampere service, but it takes only one-tenth of an ampere to kill. Be extra careful when working around sinks, tubs, and other plumbing fixtures. In addition to the added possibility of touching a pipe while touching a "hot" wire, water on your skin can add to probability of a fatal shock.

As you will see when you map your electrical system, fuse boxes and circuit breakers are often located in the cellar. Many cellars have damp floors, and others may even have some standing water. If either is the case, work must be done while standing on a wooden ladder or on a dry wood plank.

Finding the Main Switch

Before you begin your electrical map, you will have to find the main switch and power distribution panel. In general, there are three different systems in use today to shut off the main power line. Even if you have no immediate electrical work to do, you should find the main switch box and make sure that you know how to shut off the power. Knowing how to do this is just as important as knowing the fastest way out of your home in the event of a fire. And it

With this type of electrical panel you pull the main fuses completely out of the panel to shut off all current.

is the place where you will begin to draw your electrical "map."

Cartridge-type Panel   This type of panel has two plastic boxes which can be removed by pulling on the handles. The main power is completely disconnected when these boxes and the fuses which are mounted on them have been pulled out. Reactivating the circuit is simply a matter of plugging back the boxes the same way they came out. The round screw-in plug fuses which appear in this type of panel are used to control the branch circuits within the home and will be the main source of information on the map you will draw.

Circuit Breakers   To shut off the power with this system, simply flip the larger of the switches to the "off" position. When power is to be restored, reverse the procedure.

Lever Switch Panels   Lever switch panels are usually found in older homes. Just pull the lever on the box to the position marked "off" and the main line will

To cut off the current to a particular circuit, you can unscrew the plug fuse serving that circuit.

Circuit breakers are similar to switches. The large switches on top are the main breakers; the smaller switches on the bottom control individual circuits.

be dead. This type of panel usually contains plug fuses to control the branch circuits.

Drawing Your Electrical Map

Once you have located the panel and main switch, you will be ready to draw your electrical map. Once drawn, this map will not only simplify future electrical repairs; it will help when you have to replace fuses in the dark.

Drawing this map will take a little time, but it will be worth it. Begin by numbering all the fuses or circuit breakers on your panel. Then, unscrew fuse number 1 (or open circuit breaker number 1), and note which lights go out. As we mentioned earlier, a single fuse may serve different circuits in different parts of the house. If a light goes out in one room, you may not have gotten all the circuits in your record. Be sure to plug a lamp in each electrical outlet in each room, and check every outlet and fixture on your map.

When you have finished this survey, you will have accounted for every built-in light and electrical outlet and tied each to a specific fuse or circuit breaker. Keep this diagram near the fuse box, along with a flashlight. You will now be ready for electrical emergencies and be able to disconnect circuits immediately.

Replacing Fuses

The fuse is the weak link of the electrical system. It was designed to be just that. A short circuit or an overload causes excessive current to be drawn through the lines. If this situation were to reach a critical point—and there were no fuses or circuit breakers in the line—the wire would overheat and melt. If this were to happen, the chances are very good that there would be a fire. However, fuses are designed to carry only a safe amount of current. A current load beyond the rating of the fuse causes it to melt, automatically opening the circuit and protecting the wiring and the house. The melting takes place inside the fuse, where it can do no harm.

Obviously, when a fuse blows, there is a problem somewhere in the circuit. First, examine the glass window on the fuse; a blackened window indicates a short circuit, while a clear or slightly "smoky" window indicates an overload. In either case, you will see that the little metal bar inside the glass has melted and left the circuit "open." *Be sure to replace a fuse with one that has the identical amperage rating of the fuse which blew.*

Before you replace the fuse, the cause of the problem must be determined. If the fuse window has blackened, you must find the short. A short can be very dangerous and might cause a fire if it is not fixed before a new fuse is installed. If you cannot find the short in the appliances plugged into the blown circuit, the chances are that it is in the internal house wiring. Repairing such a job is a task for a licensed electrician—not for you and your seven tools.

However, there is one simple test that you can make to determine if there is actually a short in the internal house wiring. First remove all the bulbs and appliances from the circuit served by the blown fuse. Unswitching them is not enough; they must be completely removed. Then substitute a light bulb for the plug fuse in the fuse box temporarily. If the bulb lights, there is, indeed, a short in the wiring. *A licensed electrician must be called immediately. In the meantime, remove the bulb and do not replace the fuse.* This will leave the dangerous circuit in a harmless condition.

If the fuse window is clear or smoky but the bar in the window has melted, it is an overload problem. Usually, you will discover that you have put too many appliances on a single circuit. The solution is simply to unplug one of the greater-current-using appliances—such as a toaster—before replacing the fuse. The appliance can safely be plugged in another circuit protected by another fuse. Generally speaking, applainces which use heat—toasters, broilers, coffee makers, and the like—use a lot more current than motor-driven appliances such as mixers or fans.

Plug Fuses   Plug fuses are replaced by unscrewing them and screwing in a new fuse. It is a good idea to keep a box of fuses near the fuse box. Again, be sure to replace blown fuses with fuses of exactly the same rating.

Cartridge Fuses   Cartridge fuses are generally reserved for use on main incoming circuits or on lines feeding electric stoves. The only cartridge fuse you should attempt to replace is that which comes out completely on the back of the plastic box on cartridge-type panels. This fuse is then completely isolated from any electricity. The fuse can be removed from its holder by using a slip-joint pliers in

If your internal wiring contains a short circuit, the bulb will light when screwed in the fuse opening. Call an electrician at once.

the middle of the fuse. Pull out straight, and with a steady, even pressure.

Circuit Breakers   In a sense, both the cartridge and plug fuse are circuit breakers because when they burn out, they do break the circuit. But the term "circuit breaker" is reserved in home electricity for a device which automatically opens the circuit when an overload occurs, but which can be reset without the need for replacing an element. Circuit breakers resemble switches, when viewed from the front of the panel, and resetting is simply a matter of switching them to "on" again. However, the same caution applies to circuit breakers as to fuses: Before the switch is turned to "on," the source of the short or overload must be found and corrected.

There is another advantage to circuit breakers; they are all built for specific current levels. Even if one is tempted to increase current capacity, as can be done by using larger-value fuses, this can't be done with a circuit breaker.

The narrowest circuit-breaker handle controls a single circuit; a wider unit protects two lines, and a double unit with connecting handles protects 240-volt lines.

How to Calculate the Safe Limit for Home Appliances

Now that you have each fuse accounted for on your electrical map, you may want to determine just how much current you can draw from each circuit.

Fuses are always rated in amperes, but appliances may be rated either in amperes or watts. However, some very simple calculations will allow you to determine exactly how much power can be consumed before a fuse will blow. This simple formula will give you the wattage rating when you know the amperes and voltage:

Watts = voltage multiplied by amperage

For example, suppose in a 120-volt line you have an appliance which draws 2 amperes. The wattage is 2 × 120, or 240 watts.

To find amperes, use this formula:

Amperes = watts divided by voltage

For example, if you have an appliance which is rated at 200 watts and it is used on a 120-volt line, the rating would be 200 ÷ 120, or 1.6 amperes.

To determine the total number of lights and appliances which can be used safely on one fused circuit, it is only necessary to add up the total number of amperes drawn by all the electrical loads in that circuit. If this figure exceeds the rating of the fuse, the load will be too much for the line. *Do not increase the fuse rating to accommodate a greater load.* Use separate circuits for the additional appliances.

The important thing to remember is that you can rearrange loads and still have an electrically safe house. If, for example, you have a refrigerator and an air conditioner on the same circuit, you might have problems when the motor of one starts while the other is running. A motor start-up represents a momentary short circuit, and when the line is already working near capacity, it is possible to keep blowing fuses. The only solution, other than bringing in a separate line for one of the appliances (which should be done by a licensed electrician), is to move one of the units to another circuit. Whatever you do, don't try to solve the problem by using progressively heavier fuses or extension cords from other circuits. You may solve the fuse-blowing problem, but you certainly may end up starting a fire in your house wiring.

Grounding Precautions

In the United States, there are standards and codes to ensure the safe use of electricity. These codes are constantly being reviewed and revised to provide the best possible protection.

Many older homes are wired with the two-wire system we have already described. In this system, a black wire carries the current and a white wire is considered to be neutral. The white wire carries no electricity unless the circuit is energized by turning on a light or appliance. Then, electricity flows through both wires. This white wire should never touch a black wire; a short circuit will result.

During your electrical mapping you probably noticed that your fuse or circuit-breaker panel was connected to a ground rod or cold-water pipe by a heavy wire. The white wires in all home circuits are ultimately connected to the frame of the panel, and this is connected to ground for safety and power transmission reasons, as well as to reduce the possibility of damage from a lightning strike.

Newer homes are wired with a three-wire system. The third wire connects all the metal hardware in an electrical system: BX (armored) cable, switch and outlet boxes, and other exposed metal parts. This third wire is connected to a third prong on the outlet.

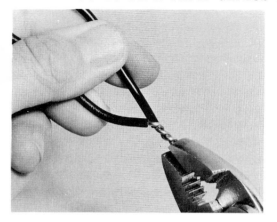

A pigtail splice. On heavier wire you will have to use your pliers.

When an appliance with a three-pronged plug is used in this outlet, the outer metal case of the appliance is internally connected to this wire, as is all the metal in the circuit right down to the grounding connection at the water pipe or ground rod. If a fault develops within the appliance and a hot wire connects with the case, a fuse will blow, rather than transmit a potentially lethal shock to the user.

The newer, nonarmored cable being used in modern homes has a third, uninsulated wire running with the other two leads. This is the safety grounding wire, and when the connections are made, it is connected to the receptacle box.

If you are concerned with electrical safety but don't want to go to the bother of installing all-new three-wire receptacles, it is possible to use grounding adapter plugs with all your three-wire appliances. It should be considered a temporary measure only.

How to Splice Wire   Joining wire to wire is called *splicing*. There are many different kinds of splices, and all but one should be left to the electrician. Don't try to join one lamp or extension cord with another by splicing and taping wires. Replace the whole length of wire for safety's sake. The only splice you will have to do when making the simple electrical

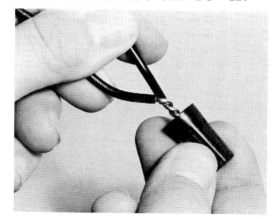

A wire nut is the fastest way to make an electrical connection.

repairs we detail in this book is joining one wire to another within an outlet or wall switch box. When internal wiring is to be joined inside a terminal or switch box, there will be no physical stress on the connection, so the *pigtail* splice, using *wire nuts*, should be used.

In most cases, the wire you will be joining will have the insulation removed, but if it becomes necessary to remove some insulation, a sharp knife should be used. Estimate how much bare wire you will need, and make a circular cut completely around the insulation. However, do not cut at right angles to the wire; this can result in nicked and weakened wire if you cut too deeply. Rather, make the cut at a slight angle toward the end of the wire, as though you were whittling a stick. When the insulation has been cut through, pull it off. It may be necessary to use the edge of the knife to get it started.

To make the wire-nut splice, hold both ends of the stripped wire side by side, and twist together. If the wire is heavy, use your pliers to get a compact twist. However, avoid overtwisting, because this can weaken or even break the wire. Once this step has been completed, the twisted wires are pushed into the open end of the wire nut, and the nut is turned until all the uninsulated wire fits snugly under the cap. If any bare wire still shows beneath the opening of the wire nut, remove the wire nut and trim the wire ends shorter so that all the uninsulated wire will be protected by the plastic wire nut.

Wire nuts should only be used inside electrical boxes—never to splice exposed cords or to make appliance connections.

SIMPLE ELECTRICAL REPAIRS YOU CAN MAKE

Replacing Burned-out Bulbs

This is, of course, the simplest of tasks, requiring only the removal and replacement of a bulb. But there are times when a broken bulb must be removed, and there is nothing to grab.

The first thing to do when removing a broken bulb is to turn off the power to the socket. There are lethal voltages in the leads to the filament, and with the glass envelope broken, it will be impossible to remove the bulb without touching the wires. Of course, if you made the electrical map we described, this part will be a snap.

With the power off, use your pliers to break away all the glass—including the inside pedestal holding the electrical leads. When the socket is clear of glass,

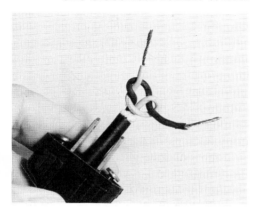

A stress-relief or underwriter's knot prevents strains on electrical connections.

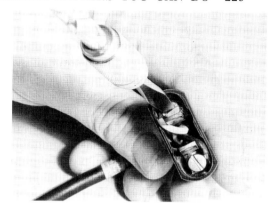

Wrap each wire around the prong of the plug, and then put the bare ends under each screw. The wire should go in the same direction as the screw is tightened.

take a dry towel and force it into the base of the bulb. When it is tightly wedged, you should be able to turn the towel in your hand, forcing the base to turn out of the socket. If the bulb base is rusted in, as sometimes happens in an outside fixture, it will be necessary to break away all the glass and the ceramic inside so that all that remains is the metal base. This is then easily collapsed with pliers and pulled out.

Repairing or Replacing an Electrical Plug

Electrical wire on appliances is stranded so that it will take considerable bending before it breaks. Such wire often fatigues at the plug, and when this happens, the plug must be removed, the wire shortened a little past the damaged area, and the plug reinstalled.

Remove the damaged wire by loosening the two screws on the underside of the plug and pulling the old wire through the hole. Then, cut the wire off evenly an inch or two from the damaged point. Pass the trimmed end through the hole in the base of the plug, and tie a stress-relief knot, as shown in the illustration. Pull the individual wires around the plug prongs, and press them into the recesses. Note the length of the wire, and add about ½ inch for the connection which will be made under each screwhead.

Cut the wire at this point, and strip off about ¼ inch of insulation with a pocket knife. Be careful when cutting through the insulation not to cut into any of the strands of the wire. Now, reposition the wire in the recesses, and fasten the stripped ends under each screwhead. Be sure to wrap the wire in the same direction as screw rotation for tightening—clockwise.

When both screws have been tightened, pull the cord into the plug, against the stress-relief knot, and firmly press the separate leads into the recesses for a neat, tight fit. If the plug had a fiber protective fire cover, it should be replaced.

Repairing an Electric Lamp

If your lamp goes out, the first thing to check is the bulb. Do this by substituting a bulb that is known to be working. If the replacement bulb doesn't work, you should then check the condition of the plug. We have already explained how to repair and replace the plug.

If both of these tests fail to turn up the cause of the problem, the chances are that solution lies in the replacement of the socket switch assembly. These assemblies are very inexpensive, and it is not worth the effort to try to repair them.

Be sure to pull the plug before you go any further.

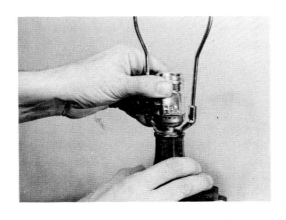

A socket shell is easily removed if you press near the word "press" engraved on the shell.

Most of these assemblies, regardless of whether a push, twist, or chain-pull switch is used, are held in place by a two-piece brass shell at the top of the lamp. Don't remove the entire assembly; it is only necessary to remove the top cap. The bulb must, of course, be removed first. To remove the top cap, look for the word "press" on the housing. Then simply press in and lift the upper housing off to expose the socket switch assembly.

First check to see if one or both of the wires has come off the screw terminals. If this is the case, tightening the screws, with the wire under them, may solve the problem. But if that fails, you will have to replace the socket. When you buy a replacement, it will not be necessary to buy an extra shell. You already have the shell in the lamp.

When connecting the new socket, wrap the wire on the screw terminals in the same direction as the turn to tighten the head—clockwise. If you haven't pulled any of the wire up from the base, the socket should fit comfortably under the brass housing. But if any extra wire has been pulled up to make the repair easier, pull it back through the bottom of the lamp.

You are now ready to replace the upper brass shell, but first make sure that the shell still has the cardboard or fiber liner inside. If not, the shell will short against the screws and may blow a fuse.

If tightening these two screws doesn't work, replace the socket assembly you see here. You can also change your lamps to accept three-way bulbs by installing a three-way socket.

Now, press the shell back into the lower half of the socket housing until it clicks in place, and your repair is complete.

In the process of replacing a socket, you may discover a dried and cracked wire inside the lamp. Being close to the head of the bulb, the insulation will crack quicker there than at any other place on the cord. If this has occurred, you should replace the entire cord.

Begin by removing the switch-socket assembly as we have described. Next, disconnect the wire from the terminals. You will have to pull this wire through the lamp, but first tie a heavy piece of string to the end of the wire at the socket. This string should be somewhat longer than the total length of the lamp and base. Now, pull the wire through the lamp from the plug end. This will leave the string inside the lamp.

Tie a new wire to the end of the string at the base of the lamp, and pull the new cord up into the socket base. You will now have to strip the insulation from the ends and attach the wire as we described in socket replacement. The chances are that the old receptacle plug will be usable. Strip the insulation from the wire, and attach the plug as we have previously explained.

After shutting off the current, remove the cover plate of defective switches or outlets.

Replacing Electrical Switches

Wall switches can fail, and they should be replaced rather than repaired. If a switch shorts out, it will blow a fuse. However, the most common cause of switch problems is simple mechanical failure. When this happens, either the switch will not move at all, or if it can be moved, it does not work.

Before any work is done on the switch, shut off the power to the circuit. Begin by removing the switch plate. This is done by removing the screws that hold it in place. With the plate off, remove the two fastening screws at the top and bottom of the switch. This will aloow you to remove the switch from the box. the switch will be held rather firmly by the connecting wires.

If the switch is controlling a single circuit, replacement will be simple. Just loosen the screws holding the wires, and install a new switch. Be sure to connect the wires to the new switch as they were connected to the faulty unit. You will notice that the wire terminals, unlike outlet terminals, are both made of brass. This is to indicate that only "hot" wires are used in the switching circuit. Ground lines

Remove the two screws to get the switch assembly out of the wall box.

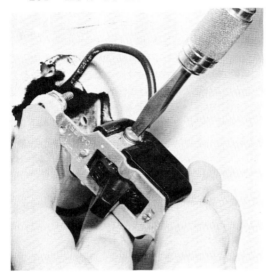

Loosen the screws holding the wires, and remove the switch. Replace with a new switch by simply reconnecting the wires. You may want to replace the switch with a silent mercury switch, or even with a dimmer switch for certain locations.

are never switched. *Note:* Make sure that you install the switch in the right position: up for "on" and down for "off."

Two-way and multiple switch units may appear complicated, but if you will note carefully just what wire went to what screw and you buy an exact replacement, you will have absolutely no trouble. Tuck the wires back in the box, position the switch, and fasten it with the screws. Then replace the switch plate and the job is done.

Replacing an Electrical Outlet

Because nothing moves inside an electrical outlet, it will seldom, if ever, need replacement. Usually failure results because a half-dozen paint jobs have sealed the contacts. To test a suspected outlet, plug in a lamp you know is working. If the fuse is OK, and the lamp switch is turned on but the bulb fails to light, you might have outlet trouble.

Replacement is similar to the job of installing a

Defective outlets are replaced in the same way as switches. Only be sure that you connect the black wires to the brass screws and the white wires to the silver-colored screws. On newer grounded outlets a green wire is connected to a green screw.

new switch. First turn off the main power at the fuse box, and then remove the outlet plate. Two screws at the top and bottom of the outlet are then removed, allowing you to pull the outlet from the box, where it can be removed from its connecting wires.

If yours is an older home, you will have only two wires to contend with. However, it is important that these two wires be replaced exactly as follows: The white wire must connect to the chrome-plated terminal and the black wire to the brass terminal of a new outlet.

Newer installations have a third wire, as we described, which is connected to the back of the electrical box. This is the grounding wire, and it must be connected to the green terminal on the outlet. There are situations with switches and outlets where more than one wire is connected to a terminal. When replacing these units, reconnect each wire exactly as it was installed on the original switch or outlet. Even if you are not an artist, a simple sketch of the original connections will help your memory when replacing wires.

Inspecting for Loose Wires

Wires connecting appliances to plugs can weaken from use, become frayed, or work loose from the screws or connectors which hold them. All these conditions can be bothersome and often very dangerous. It pays to make periodic check of all the cords in your house.

Begin by making a visual inspection, checking for frayed insulation along the full length of the wire. When a wire has been rubbing on something, there might be a break in the insulation. At the point where the wire enters the appliance or plug, there is a strong possibility of wear.

Wear at the plug can be remedied by shortening the wire and replacing the plug, as we have already described. But where wear is further along the line, it is best to replace the wire completely.

Wire can work loose from screw terminals and other connectors. Check for this problem by jiggling the wire with the appliance turned on. If there is a loose wire, you will know it by the intermittent operation of the appliance. This wire should be replaced if it is worn or if many strands are broken. If it is only a matter of loose terminals, simply tightening the connections will often solve the problem.

Older wire was made with rubber insulation, which has relatively short life. When this insulation dries out, it can crack and break off. Such wire should be replaced. Newer insulations are made of plastic with a longer life and greater flexing ability.

Repairing Bells and Transformers

Doorbells and chimes run on low voltage which is derived from a transformer. The output of these transformers seldom exceeds 20 volts. This low volt-

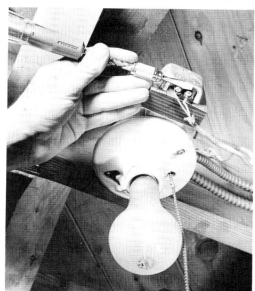

A bell transformer is often mounted directly on some convenient electrical box. Harmless low-voltage terminals are exposed and generally clearly marked 20 volts or less. To test the transformer, touch a screwdriver blade across the terminals. A small spark indicates a good transformer.

age is not dangerous, but the power into the transformer is still 120 volts, and it is lethal. It is safe to work on the low-voltage side of a bell transformer without shutting off the power.

When a bell, buzzer or chime fails to respond to the pushing of a button, the problem often lies right at the button. Push buttons are outside and are exposed to the weather; contacts pit and corrode, losing their ability to pass current. Often it is enough to remove the button, brighten up the contacts with sandpaper, and put the button back for a few more years' use. But if the contacts are beyond this, it is best to replace the entire push button.

If, when the button is removed, and you touch the two bare wires together and the bell doesn't sound, you have another problem. It could be a loose or broken wire, a defective transformer, or a defective bell. Fortunately, each of these problems is easy to isolate.

Connect short wires to your bell or chimes after removing the assembly from your wall. Then take the assembly to the transformer and see if you get a sound. If you get no sound and your transformer tests all right, you will have to repair or replace the bell. If you get a sound, something is wrong with the wiring between transformer and chime.

Before you do any extensive wire tracing, follow the leads to the bell and transformer. Jiggle to test and then tighten all connections. If this fails to restore the bell, test the transformer by briefly placing a screwdriver blade across the low-voltage wires coming *from the transformer.* You should see a very weak spark. *Note:* Make sure that you select the wires going to the bell and button, *not* the wire from the house lines to the transformer. There are lethal voltages on this side of the transformer. Sometimes the transformer is connected directly to a junction box so that the 110-volt wires are not exposed.

If you get the spark, go on to check the bell itself. Remove the bell and take it to the transformer. Then get two short pieces of wire and connect the bell directly to the low-voltage side of the transformer. If it doesn't ring, the bell is faulty. If it does ring, the fault lies in the wiring between the transformer and the doorbell button.

If the bell is faulty, either you can replace it with a new unit, or you might want to tinker with it first. If you can open the case, look for an assembly which consists of a coil of wire and an armature to which the bell is attached. This armature will have a set of electrical contacts near the end of the coil. Try cleaning the contacts with fine sandpaper. This often restores service, saving the cost of a new bell. But if it doesn't, you might as well buy a replacement.

Now, if you have found that the problem is in the wiring, you may have to replace it all. If a lot of the bell wire is stapled inside walls, the job can be burdensome. You might try replacing the wiring by leaving the old wire in place and simply running new lengths of wire in more easily accessible places. Look first and see if old wire has been damaged some place and can be repaired.

Repairing Fluorescent Lights

Compared with a conventional incandescent bulb, a fluorescent light will last many thousands of hours longer. In fact, the fluorescent tube benefits from being left on. Manufacturers rate the life of a fluorescent tube by the number of times it is turned on and off, rather than by hours of illumination as they do with incandescent bulbs.

Basically, there are three major parts to a fluorescent light: the *tube*, the *starter*, and the *ballast*.

Straight fluorescent tubes are installed by placing the pins at both ends in the sockets and sliding them along one side of the socket. The second set of pins will enter the bottom of the socket groove and follow the track along the other side of the socket. A slight turning motion as the tube is installed will engage the pins with a spring clip, and the tube will be held firmly in place. Circular tubes have pins in the middle which fit into a plug in the fixture. The tube itself is held in place with little spring clips. Replacement of the starter is handled by pressing the new starter down in the socket and giving it a quarter turn.

Compared with an incandescent bulb, which is either working or burned out, there are quite a few things that can go wrong with a fluorescent light. Here are some of the major problems and their cures.

Flickering Light   If the tube is new, this is a common condition and will disappear after a few hours of use. With an older tube, the best solution is to replace the starter. When both of these remedies fail, the ballast will have to be replaced. However, this is not a job for you and your seven simple tools. Call a licensed electrician to do the job.

Tube Does Not Light   First, check the fuse or circuit breaker; then try replacing the starter. If these remedies fail, try replacing the tube. If all these tests fail, the ballast is at fault, and, again, this is a job for a licensed electrician.

Short Tube Life   If the fixture is turned on and off frequently, the tube life will be greatly shortened. If this is not the case, the starter should be replaced. If this does not do the trick, have an electrician replace the ballast.

Blinking Light   First, check to make sure that the tube is properly seated in its socket. Check the condition of the tube pins. It is often possible to bend the pins during installation, causing intermittent contact with the power. While you have the tube out, you might brighten up the pins by lightly rubbing fine sandpaper on them. If these operations don't help, the problem most likely lies with the ballast.

Discolored Tube Ends   A little brown at the ends of the tube is normal, but if a black color appears in a new tube, the starter should be replaced. Discoloration at one end can be remedied by simply reversing the tube in its socket.

THE USE AND ABUSE OF EXTENSION CORDS

An extension cord is a handy way to get power where you need it when an outlet is not nearby. But unless the cord is properly sized for the load, you will have problems. Using a long extension cord may result in a considerable voltage drop at the end of the line. This can cause problems at the appliance being used at the end of the cord, and it can blow fuses. Also, the size of the wire is a factor in its current-carrying capacity, and any extension cord should be matched to the appliance it will serve.

Extension cords are commonly sold in hardware and other types of stores. However, often the people in these stores will be unable to help you decide if the cord will be able to do the job. So, use this rule of thumb: Extension cords made of the same cord as those feeding lamps, table radios, and other small appliances should be used only for similar appliances. Because an extension cord may have three outlets on it, don't be fooled into thinking that it will be possible to power three heavy-duty appliances.

When buying an extension cord for heavy-duty appliances, such as power tools, go to an electrical supply store and tell the clerk just what kind of tool will be fed with the line. He or she can then give you an extension cord with a margin of safety. Be sure also that the cord has the seal of the Underwriter's Laboratory.

Extension cords should never be used as a substitute for house wiring. If an appliance is to be located in an area where there is no outlet, the extension cord can be a temporary solution, but you should consider either adding another outlet at the spot (have an electrician do the job), or using one of the surface-mounted lines that you can install yourself.

INSTALLING SURFACE WIRING

Some rooms are wired with too few outlets, or the placement of the outlets is inconvenient for the furniture and appliance layout. It is tempting to use extension cords, but they are unsightly and unsafe for permanent use. A better solution lies in the installation of wall surface wiring. This easy-to-install wiring will eliminate your octopus problems and put electricity where you need it. But it is important to remember that by doing this, you are not adding extra circuits—you are only extending the reach of existing wiring. Therefore, you will not be able to increase the number of appliances which can be used with the circuit. If the line feeding the outlet you plan to use to feed the surface wiring carries 20 amperes, you will not increase the capacity to 40 amperes by adding another outlet.

However, because all appliances on a single circuit are seldom on at one time, you probably will have no problems with some minor additions to the line. The conductors in some commercial surface wiring systems will carry 20 amperes, but if the circuit to which you connect the new line is rated at only 15 amperes, you will be able to draw only 15 amperes.

Basically, there are two major types of surface wiring. One type is installed in metal raceways and must be connected internally with existing house wiring. If you have any electrical skills, you might attempt this system. But the most easily installed systems are attached to the wall or baseboard and then are connected by simply plugging in as you would with any other extension cord. There are a variety of different systems, and threaded light sockets are available as well as the conventional plug-in outlets. Be sure to look for UL approval on the equipment before you buy.

One system of flexible plastic cable can be cut wherever it is desired to splice the outlets. Another is a combination of flexible and rigid plastic strips which plug together end-to-end, eliminating the need to cut and strip wire. A third system is basically a flat plastic ribbon or track that allows the user to insert or remove outlets at any point. Again, UL approval is important.

Because there are so many different types of wall-mounted wiring systems, it is difficult to give detailed instructions for their use. Manufacturers include explicit instructions with each kit. There are, however, a few basic considerations that it will be important to understand before you select a system.

If the system is to be used only on one flat surface, the rigid plastic strip is the best to use. If the wiring is to go around corners, the system you select must have provision for bends. Try to plan the run of wire in an inconspicuous place; most of these lines are run along the baseboard, or sometimes on the wall just above the baseboard.

These handy wiring systems provide an easy way to get electricity to out-of-the-way places. Their use should not be overdone. If you need a lot of extra outlets, it's a sign your house is underwired and professional advice should be sought.

There's More You Can Do . . .

This chapter was written to explain the basics of an electrical system and to guide you in doing the simple repairs that can cost so much when done by a professional. Even if you have no knowledge of electricity, you should be able to handle most of the electrical problems that you will normally encounter.

But if you want to do more than repairs—add wall outlets, outdoor lights, or additional circuits, for example—you should consult a licensed electrician.

APPENDIX

Lumber

The best source of help in choosing the correct grade and type of lumber is your local dealer. You can make fairly ambitious projects quite easily with your simple tools if you let the lumberyard do most of the cutting operations for you. For a nominal charge they will cut lumber and plywood to your specifications. Simple bookcases, cabinets, and similar storage units can be designed for such precutting and then assembled with a hammer or screwdriver. Two cautions are in order: First, keep all cuts simple. Straight, square dimensions are best. Second, make sure you know exactly how thick and wide standard boards run. You will recall that actual and nominal sizes do not coincide. This table will help you. All dimensions are inches.

Nominal Size What You Order	Actual Size What You Get
1 x 2	$\frac{3}{4}$ x $1\frac{1}{2}$
1 x 4	$\frac{3}{4}$ x $3\frac{1}{2}$
1 x 6	$\frac{3}{4}$ x $5\frac{1}{2}$
1 x 8	$\frac{3}{4}$ x $7\frac{1}{4}$
1 x 10	$\frac{3}{4}$ x $9\frac{1}{4}$
1 x 12	$\frac{3}{4}$ x $11\frac{1}{4}$
2 x 2	$1\frac{9}{16}$ x $1\frac{9}{16}$
2 x 3	$1\frac{9}{16}$ x $2\frac{9}{16}$
2 x 4	$1\frac{9}{16}$ x $3\frac{9}{16}$
2 x 6	$1\frac{9}{16}$ x $5\frac{5}{8}$
2 x 8	$1\frac{9}{16}$ x $7\frac{1}{2}$
2 x 10	$1\frac{9}{16}$ x $9\frac{1}{2}$
2 x 12	$1\frac{9}{16}$ x $11\frac{1}{2}$

Standard lengths of lumber run from 8 to 16 feet in increments of 2 feet.

Plywood

There are many different grades of plywood, each designed for a specific use. Most lumberyards carry a few popular grades and will special-order anything out of the ordinary. Here are some useful facts to remember:

Size and Thickness Available   The standard-size plywood sheet is 4 by 8 feet. Some yards will sell half and quarter sheets. The minimum thickness is ³⁄₁₆ inch. The rest increase by ⅛-inch increments: ¼, ⅜, ½, ⅝, and ¾ inch.

Selecting for Use and Appearance   Plywood comes in interior and exterior grades. The exterior grade is constructed with waterproof glue and will stand exposure to weather. It is also more expensive. The highest-quality surface is graded A, while grade D permits quite a few large knotholes. For natural-finished cabinet work you will choose the best grade for appearance. Rough work can use lesser grades.

Nails

Nails, you will remember, are described by *penny* length, usually abbreviated *d*. The following table gives nail sizes and the approximate number of common nails per pound.

Size	Length in Inches	Number per Pound
2d	1	875
3d	1¼	550
4d	1½	300
5d	1¾	250
6d	2	175
8d	2½	100
10d	3	70
12d	3¼	60
16d	3½	45
20d	4	30

When nailing two pieces of wood together, choose a length that will go through the first piece and at least halfway into the second piece of wood.

Screws

Wood screws commonly come with round or flat heads. Flat heads require an additional operation called *countersinking* so the head of the screw will rest flush with the surface. When two boards are joined, a hole is drilled big enough in the first board to clear the body of the screw. A smaller pilot hole is drilled in the second board so that the screw will enter the wood without splitting it. Here are common sizes of screws and drill sizes for the pilot holes. The smaller sizes can be handled with the drill points that come with your spiral-ratchet screwdriver.

Gauge Number of Screw	Body Diameter	Pilot Hole
2	.086	$3/64$
4	.112	$1/16$
5	.125	$5/64$
6	.138	$5/64$
7	.151	$3/32$
8	.164	$3/32$
9	.177	$7/64$
10	.190	$7/64$
12	.216	$1/8$
14	.242	$9/64$

INDEX